# THE ULTIMATE
# BOOK OF MAGIC
# AND WITCHCRAFT

## A How-To Book on the Practice of Magic Rituals and Spells

## PIERRE MACEDO

The Ultimate Book of Magic and Witchcraft: A How-To Book on the Practice of Magic Rituals and Spells © 2017 by Pierre Macedo. All rights reserved. No part of this book may be used or reproduced in any manner whatsoever, including internet usage, without written permission from Leirbag Press, except in the case of brief quotations embodied in critical articles and reviews.

ISBN: 978-0-9959742-0-3 (Paperback)
ISBN: 978-0-9959742-1-0 (Hardcover)
ISBN: 978-0-9959742-2-7 (E-book)

First Edition 2017

Published by Leirbag Press, an imprint of Virgo Publishers.
contact@virgopublishers.com

## Before You Begin Your Reading

Twelve chapters are part of this book, and I advise the reader to read them all in the order they are presented here. The concepts and techniques introduced and detailed in a chapter, are not explained again in the following sections. Reading the entire book is the best way to make the most of it.

Pierre Macedo

# Contents

INTRODUCTION ................................................................. xi

GENERAL INSTRUCTIONS ................................................. 1
    Self-Preparation ............................................................. 1
    The Temple Arrangement ............................................. 3
    Casting and Closing a Circle ......................................... 4
    Consecrating Objects .................................................... 6
    Seals of the Spirits ........................................................ 8

BREAKING AND CLEANSING SPELLS ............................. 9
    Breaking Spells and Removing Negative Energies ...... 10
    Space Cleansing .......................................................... 12
    Spell-Breaking Amulet ............................................... 13
    Ritual of the Pentagram ............................................. 17

LOVE SPELLS .................................................................... 23
    Love Spell 01 ............................................................... 24
    Love Spell 02: Working with Lilith ............................ 27
    Love Spell 03: Working with Baal .............................. 31
    Love Spell 04: Working with Aphrodite .................... 34

BEAUTY SPELLS .............................................................. 39
    Frey and Freya ............................................................ 40
    Aphrodite .................................................................... 49

MONEY SPELLS ............................................................... 53
    Working with Bune ..................................................... 54

    Working with Seere ................................................................ 56

MANIPULATION SPELL ................................................................. 59

    Working with Belial ................................................................ 60

FINDING ANSWERS ...................................................................... 63

    The Name of Your Guardian Angel and Demon ..................... 64

    Getting Answers from a Deck of Cards ................................. 71

    Free Writing .............................................................................. 75

EVOCATIONS ................................................................................ 77

    Lucifer ....................................................................................... 78

    Michael ..................................................................................... 83

    Lilith .......................................................................................... 88

PLANETARY MAGIC ..................................................................... 93

    The Seven Planets and Their Characteristics ....................... 94

    Power Hierarchy ...................................................................... 98

    Evoking Planetary Spirits ...................................................... 101

    The Seven Olympic Spirits ................................................... 106

    Creating Planetary Seals ....................................................... 114

SELF-PROTECTION ..................................................................... 125

    Balancing Your Energy .......................................................... 126

    Amulets ................................................................................... 129

CREATING YOUR OWN RITUALS AND SPELLS ...................... 133

    Step by Step ............................................................................ 134

COMMON QUESTIONS AND SOLUTIONS .............................. 137

APPENDIX ................................................................................... 141

Invoking and Banishing the Four Elements ........................................141
Developing Your Sensitive Abilities ............................................... 143

# Figures and Tables

| | |
|---|---:|
| Figure 1. Traditional witch altar | 4 |
| Figure 2. The Banishing Pentagram of Earth | 20 |
| Figure 3. The seal of Lilith | 29 |
| Figure 4. Frey | 41 |
| Figure 5. Freya | 42 |
| Figure 6. The hammer sign | 43 |
| Figure 7. The Algiz position | 44 |
| Figure 8. The seal of Bune | 55 |
| Figure 9. The seal of Belial | 61 |
| Figure 10. Ouija Board | 68 |
| Figure 11. Playing card | 74 |
| Figure 12. Cutting the deck | 75 |
| Figure 13. The seal of Lucifer | 82 |
| Figure 14. The Invoking Pentagram of Fire | 86 |
| Figure 15. The seal of Michael | 87 |
| Figure 16. The seal of Saturn | 102 |
| Figure 17. The seal of Jupiter | 102 |
| Figure 18. The seal of Mars | 102 |
| Figure 19. The seal of the Sun | 102 |
| Figure 20. The seal of Venus | 102 |
| Figure 21. The seal of Mercury | 102 |
| Figure 22. The seal of the Moon | 102 |
| Figure 23. The seals of Agiel and Zazel | 102 |
| Figure 24. The seals of Yophiel and Hismael | 103 |
| Figure 25. The seals of Graphiel and Bartzabel | 103 |
| Figure 26. The seals of Nakhiel and Sorath | 103 |
| Figure 27. The seals of Hagiel and Qedemel | 103 |
| Figure 28. The seals of Tiriel and Taphthartharath | 103 |
| Figure 29. The seals of the Intelligence of the Moon and Chasmodai | 104 |
| Figure 30. The seal of Aratron | 108 |
| Figure 31. The seal of Bethor | 108 |
| Figure 32. The seal of Phaleg | 109 |

| | |
|---|---|
| Figure 33. The seal of Och | 109 |
| Figure 34. The seal of Hagith | 109 |
| Figure 35. The seal of Ophiel | 110 |
| Figure 36. The seal of Phul | 110 |
| Figure 37. Drawing a planetary seal | 120 |
| Figure 38. Finishing a planetary seal | 120 |
| Figure 39. The Third Pentacle of Jupiter | 130 |
| Figure 40. The Sixth Pentacle of Jupiter | 131 |
| Figure 41. The Fourth Pentacle of the Moon | 132 |
| Figure 42. Invoking and banishing pentagrams | 142 |

| | |
|---|---|
| Table 1. Pronunciation guide | 21 |
| Table 2. Pendulum | 66 |
| Table 3. The characteristics of the planets | 96 |
| Table 4. Names of the planets in Hebrew | 97 |
| Table 5. Planets and spheres | 97 |
| Table 6. Powers ruling the planets 1 | 99 |
| Table 7. Powers ruling the planets 2 | 100 |
| Table 8. Planetary incense | 104 |
| Table 9. The Olympic Spirits and their planets | 111 |
| Table 10. Flashing colors | 111 |
| Table 11. The square of Saturn | 115 |
| Table 12. The square of Jupiter | 116 |
| Table 13. The square of Mars | 116 |
| Table 14. The square of the Sun | 116 |
| Table 15. The square of Venus | 117 |
| Table 16. The square of Mercury | 117 |
| Table 17. The square of the Moon | 117 |
| Table 18. The Agrippa Gematria | 119 |

# INTRODUCTION

I came up with the idea of writing this book based on my difficulties in learning the occult arts. When I realized that I could have greater control over my life through magic, I decided that I would start studying the subject to put it into practice as soon as possible. I just didn't imagine it would be so hard to find the right sources of information, but the first step had already been taken, and there was no turning back.

Since magic is a vast topic, there are hundreds of books that address different techniques, most of which contain a lot of theory and little practice. The student who wants to delve into the subject needs to read a lot of content before they can begin to apply that knowledge in their lives. Thinking about it, I decided to create a book that was straight to the point, allowing the reader to use what they are learning immediately.

The Ultimate Book of Magic and Witchcraft features a variety of spells and magic rituals for different areas, such as love, money, beauty, manipulation, evocations, etc. All the spells presented here are unique to this book. If you are a beginner, this book is right for you because the language used is easy to understand, and everything is explained in detail. If you are familiar with magic, you will find here new techniques that will allow you to get ahead or fix what is not working for you. Therefore, I define this project as practical and advanced, yet suitable to be read by anyone who wishes to introduce the mysteries of magic and witchcraft in their lives.

You will notice that I make use of both words magician and witch. In general, there is no difference between them. The problem is that many magic practitioners don't like being called a witch. But I can assure you that real magicians are few and far between, and they don't need spells and evocations to achieve their goals because they have their own powers.

The primary focus of this book is white magic, although it contains love and manipulation spells that can't be categorized other than black magic. The difference between these two terms is the intention of the practitioner. If you want to attract something into your life without directly causing harm to anyone, this is white magic. On the contrary, if you explicitly want to change the course of someone's life, this is black magic. Many, including myself, believe in something called karma that consists of reaping what you sow. If you do good things to others, that is what you will receive in this or the next life. It is up to you to decide which way you should go.

It is important to say, from the moment you start walking this path, you truly have to believe it, so that everything can work effectively. Your mind has the power of doing two essential things: to break magic spells and manifest your intentions. This applies in particular when we are working without the help of any spiritual beings. This type of spell is highly dependent on the magician or witch subconscious, while the ones cast with the help of some entity will depend more on the entity itself.

All the spells were carefully prepared, mixing ancient and modern magic. Although we don't need to do all the hard work our ancestors used to do, we can't completely get rid of some necessary steps, such as body and soul purification. These can dictate the success of our work because when doing magic, we are dealing with higher forces that don't share our human characteristics responsible for making us impure beings.

Now you have in your hands the key to change the course of your life. Use it wisely. I wish you good luck on your magical journey. May the universe conspire in your favor.

# CHAPTER 1

# GENERAL INSTRUCTIONS

Let's start with some basic instructions that all those who wish to become an initiate must know. Many aspiring magicians and witches ignore these steps for sheer lack of knowledge or because they want to do things more quickly, but some think they are already very experienced and no longer need to stick to acts that must precede any ritual. Not consecrating an altar for example, is disrespectful to the energy you expect to receive there. Using a wand or other magical object without proper preparation is the same as using nothing. In the same way that you prepare to receive visitors from the physical world in your home, you should also prepare to receive visitors from the astral plane.

## Self-Preparation

You are probably reading this book because you don't want what most of the other books usually bring. You want a fast way to start using the main witchcraft techniques, and this is exactly what you will get. I promise I will not teach you long fundamentals of magic, but I must say you can't skip or at least you should not skip some self-preparation before casting a spell or performing other magical acts. For the sake of good results, I am going to show you how to align yourself with the highest forces in the universe so that your magical work can receive the necessary energy it needs to bring the desired outcome.

First, you have to bear in mind that your energy will affect all your spells and rituals. It is not a possibility; it will happen for sure. In this case, we have to guarantee this influence is positive instead of leading our work to its failure. Your emotional state will not dictate the course of your spells, but it can function either giving more power for them to complete their tasks faster or building a barrier that will prevent them from passing.

One thing that is mandatory while using magic is to believe it will work. It is not just because our mind has the power of changing reality if we strongly believe that something will happen; it is because of the barrier that I mentioned in the previous paragraph as well. When you doubt it even for a second, you are putting obstacles in your aura that will cause any spell to work slowly or even stop working. So, make sure that you just don't believe it might work, but be confident that it will bring you good results.

Meditating before a ritual may help you to channel your anger, sadness, or any other strong feeling that is driving your actions, to the astral field where your magical operation will take place or to the entity in case you are working with the help of spirits. As you can see, it doesn't matter what your emotional state is at the time of the ritual. Of course, you can't be entirely happy if you are trying to bring someone you lost back; otherwise, you would not need any of it. It is just a matter of transforming these feelings into fuel that will provide extra power so that your wishes can be fulfilled.

There is also an exercise similar to meditation that can be used to channel energy to the main object utilized in a ritual. It is simple and must be made minutes before or during the magical operation. Just close your eyes and concentrate on the things you want to change in your life. Visualize it becoming a reality and then slowly turning into an abstract white or yellow light. Through your imagination, send this light to the object you are holding in your hands.

Your spiritual and physical body must also be prepared before you can contact the other side. Going without eating meat and having sex for at least 24 hours will purify your soul. Take a bath to cleanse your body, and wear clean clothes. It is a sign of respect to the spirit you will work with.

# The Temple Arrangement

A temple is a place where all magical operations are performed. It can be a bedroom, room, garden, etc. No matter wherever it is, it must be a sacred and inviolate place during the ritual. In other words, it is where you establish a connection with the universe for a higher purpose in your life. This is why it must be quiet where no one will interrupt you.

Temples can be well decorated with many candles, incense, a beautiful altar, rugs, colorful cloths, etc., or simple ones with only an altar. In fact, the altar is the only thing you should always have in your temple. It doesn't need to be a big one. It can be made with a box for example, but what matters is that it must represent the place from where the energy of your work is released to the cosmos and also where you receive the power from the cosmos. For example, if you are working with evocations, the spirit should manifest on the altar, and your offerings should be made there as well.

The temple must be open and closed. You open the temple right before you perform the first act that generally is a prayer or an invocation, and close it right after you finish casting a spell or thanking the forces that helped you. Closing the temple is a polite way of telling the spirits they should go now because the work is done.

Figure 1. Traditional witch altar

# Casting and Closing a Circle

A magic circle is a sacred place in which you should stay inside while performing a rite. It is a representation of your universe which no one is allowed to enter. While inside of a circle, you represent the center of the universe, a divine force, literally the boss. Ideally, this is how you should feel, especially when working with evocations, but it takes time to master it, and for now, you just need to understand the concept.

Depending on your level of concentration, you can choose between using a physical circle or an imaginary one. In magic, the most important thing is that everything we do is inside us. If you imagine there is a circle around you, and you strongly believe it is actually there, the effect is the same as if you had drawn one on the ground. It is up to you to decide what is best for you.

Not all magicians use circles. Many consider they are well experienced and don't need one anymore. On the contrary, it is widely used by witches and almost mandatory for any magical operation. Since this is a book with a lot of spells, you will learn the ways of casting a circle.

## Using Chalk

This method is very practical because you can easily clean the floor after you finish using the circle. Just take a piece of chalk, go to the east, and moving clockwise trace a circle wide enough for you to stay seated inside it. While doing it, you must say the following words:

> *I cast this circle to be used in my magical operation. No force is allowed to enter inside it, especially the negative ones. This is a sacred place, and it represents the universe where I am the center. So mote it be.*

After the ritual is complete, you must close the circle before you leave it. You do this by undoing it counterclockwise, starting in the east.

## Using a Wand

If you have a wand, you can use it to trace an astral circle. I said astral because it will not be visible to you unless you are tracing it in the sand or soil, but it will be active on the astral plane. If you don't have a wand, you can use your index finger. Say the same words used in the previous method. You must also close it after the work is done.

# Consecrating Objects

All objects used in spells or other magic rituals should be purified and consecrated before used. Knife, wand, pendulum, candles are some of them. For each item, there are complicated and easy manners of doing that. Both work perfectly, so we are going to focus only on the easy to medium methods.

## Consecrating Water

Water is used to consecrate magical objects, but you need to consecrate it as well.

Take a cup, glass or another container with water, place one of your hands above it, and say:

> *Creature of water, I exorcise you and cleanse you for my purpose. You are now holy, and holy will become everything you touch. Amen.*

## Consecrating and Activating the Triangle of the Art

The triangle is a perfect symbol of manifestation. It is used when we want some energy to manifest, such as spirits, for example. You can make it by almost anything, such as chalk, crayon, sticks, paper.

Place or draw the triangle on the altar or wherever you will use it, and say:

> *Triangle of the Art, I consecrate you and activate you now. You are ready to assist me in my magical work helping the higher forces of the universe to manifest in this temple.*

You must make this process every time you use a triangle. After you finish using it, say:

> *Triangle of the Art, you have served me well. Your work is done.*

## Consecrating the Altar

As explained, the altar is the place where you release the energy of your spells and also where you receive the powers involved with it. It must be consecrated with water, incense, or salt. You must say the following words:

*In the name of Tetragrammaton, I exorcise and cleanse this altar so that it can be part of this rite.*

Instead of Tetragrammaton, you can consecrate the altar in the name of the entity that will be part of your rite. For example, if you are working with the Greek goddess Hecate, use her name.

## Consecrating Any Object to the Four Elements

This is one of my favorite ways of consecrating objects like wands, pendulums, Tarot, etc. It is straightforward and efficient.

**Step by step**

I. You will need a bowl or glass of water to represent the water element. This water must be consecrated. You will also need salt or soil to represent earth, incense for air, and a candle for fire. Incense can also be used to represent fire, and your own breath, the air.

II. You may cast a circle if you want.

III. Put the incense in the east, the candle in the south, the water in the west, and the salt or soil in the north.

IV. Go to the east, facing east and holding the object you want to consecrate, say:

*I chose this [insert the name of the object] to assist me on my magical journey. So mote it be.*

V. Still in the east, burn the incense, and pass the object through the smoke while saying:

*May the powers of the air purify and consecrate this [insert the name of the object].*

VI. Repeat the same process with the other elements in their respective directions, moving clockwise east, south, west, and north. Take care when working with fire. You don't want to damage your object or get burn. The same advice is valid when working with water. Water can damage objects, especially if it is a paper made one.

VII. After finishing with the earth element in the north, return to the east, and thank the elementals that assisted you in this work. Say:

*I thank the elementals of the air, fire, water, and earth for assisting me in this work. I now declare this temple closed.*

See Chapter 2 for a more elaborate version of this consecration ritual.

# Seals of the Spirits

Seals or sigils are a set of characters representing a spirit. It is like their identity but works like a phone number you can use to call them. Seals are mostly used in evocations, and once they are activated, they represent a connection with the spirit. When you decide you no longer want to work with a certain entity, you first tell the seal it has no power anymore, and then burn it. In the following chapters, some seals are presented, such as Lucifer's, Michael's, etc.

**CHAPTER 2**

# BREAKING AND CLEANSING SPELLS

The first set of spells we are going to learn in this book are the ones you need to know before you start casting your owns. A magician or witch must know how to break any spell or to repel any negative energy because if you are targeting someone, you can also be targeted. When you enter into the occult world, it is like you are sending a message saying you are now part of that. It can be good because you attract to yourself the solutions for your problems that you could not see before, but it can be bad as well because you are also attracting forces that don't want to see you well. Let's look at how we can handle this.

# Breaking Spells and Removing Negative Energies

This spell is a powerful one and is used to remove all the negativity from your life, including black magic. So, if you think that someone has cursed you or put a black magic spell on you, this is what you need. We will be working with the fire element and its ruler, the Archangel Michael.

## Things You Will Need

- Two white candles.
- Incense (frankincense, orange, acacia, or calendula).
- Bible.

## Step by Step

### Purifying the place / Banishing with the fire element

I. Set up an altar in the south with the two candles and the incense. During this operation, you must always be facing south.

II. Hold one of the candles, light it, and say before the flame:

*Hekas hekas este bebeloi.*[1] *Far, far from this place, be the profane.*

III. Place your hand above the flame and say:

*Creature of fire, I consecrate you and awaken you immediately. I purify this flame so that it can expand and remove all negativity, and bless everything it touches.*

IV. Close your eyes and visualize the flame getting bigger and cleansing the space with the fire element. Then, quickly pass your hands through the flame to purify[2] yourself and say:

*I invite all harmful forces to leave right now. By the creature of fire, may this place be blessed and I purified. May the salamanders burn those who try to come back. I now proclaim the sacred silence.*

V. Stay in silence for a moment visualizing the place being cleansed.

**Prayer to the Archangel Michael**

I. Burn the incense.

II. Light the other candle. Vibrate[3] the name of Michael for a moment and concentrate on his energy. Say:

*O Mighty and Powerful Archangel Michael, you who carries a flaming sword that fears all enemies, you who are a faithful protector of the Divine, you who reigns over the fiery flames of the fire element. I ask you to grant me the protection I need at this moment, so that all those who attempt some evil against me, may know the fury of him who is the Prince of the Archangels. If I am not worthy at this moment, make me worthy because I choose you as a guide on this journey of physical and spiritual strengthening. My mind is open to receive all the advice and teachings you have to offer me. May my aura be surrounded by your energy as a barrier that shields against all sorts of evil. The spiritual enemies, who now hear me, fear your power because they know they will suffer the consequences of trying to attack a protégé of yours. Hail Archangel Michael. Amen.*

**Invoking Michael**

I. Say:

*O Mighty and Powerful Archangel Michael, I invoke you. Michael, Prince of the Archangels, Prince of Virtues, Prince of Light, Guardian of Peace, Protector of the Divine, Ruler of Fire, I invoke you. I ask you, O Powerful Michael, to cleanse my energy field of all the influences that may be hindering and preventing the achievement of my goals. I ask you to break and cast away all kinds of witchcraft thrown at* me. *Before this flame of the fire element, I ask you to open all the paths that are closed in my life. So mote it be. Hail beloved Archangel Michael. Amen.*

II. Recite the Psalm 85 to Michael; recite the Psalm 7 to finish the purification.

III. Thank the spirits:

*I thank the fire elementals who participated in this purification. I thank you for your presence and your help, O Mighty Archangel Michael, and I say: see you soon.*

IV. Stay in silence and put out the candles.

V. Let the incense burn to the end in a place without risk of fire

VI. You should lie down for 30 minutes after the ritual.

# Space Cleansing

Easily cleanse your home or any place of negative energies.

## Things You Will Need

- A glass of cold water with three teaspoons of salt.
- Incense (jasmine, poppy, myrtle, or sandalwood).

## Step by Step

I. First, say:

*Hekas hekas este bebeloi. Far, far from this place, be the profane.*

II. Place your hand above the glass of water and say:

*Creature of water, I consecrate you and awaken you immediately. I purify the essence of this fluid so that it can expel and remove all negativity, and bless everything it touches.*

III. Sprinkle the space in which you are purifying with the consecrated water while saying:

> *I invite all harmful forces to leave right now. By the creature of water, may this place be blessed and I purified. I now proclaim the sacred silence.*

IV. Stay in silence for a moment visualizing the place being cleansed. Concentrate on a violet flame cleansing and taking away all negative energy.

V. Burn the incense, and holding it, walk around the place while saying:

> *If there is any evil spirit here, leave now and go back to where you came from. I will not have mercy on you.*
>
> *This is my place, and those who are not invited to be here will burn and disappear without a trace.*

VI. Let the incense burn to the end in a place without risk of fire

# Spell-Breaking Amulet

Amulets are objects commonly used for protection, but they can have other uses, such as luck, love, money, etc. In the last chapter, you have access to powerful ancient amulets that will prevent you from receiving any kind of evil energy. Our first objective with this tool is to create a custom amulet that will absorb all sorts of magic cast against you. If you suspect someone cursed or hexed you, this tool is right for you. Bear in mind what we are going to create is not only a simple inanimate object but a living entity that will work on the astral plane doing exactly what it was told at the time of its creation. You must destroy it as soon as its task is complete.

## Things You Will Need

- A crystal, stone, pendant, coin, ring, etc. Choose one of these or another similar object.
- Salt.
- A glass of water.
- A white candle.
- Incense (any type).

## Step by Step

**Banishing**

Let's cleanse the temple.

I. Burn an incense stick, and holding it, go to the east and say:

> I invoke the guardians of the east to assist me in this rite. May the powers of the air cleanse this place of all negativity and evil spirits.

II. Walk around the place holding the incense and say:

> I command all harmful and evil forces to leave right now.
>
> By the powers of the air, I exorcise and purify this place.

III. Close your eyes and imagine the place being purified.

**The ritual**

I. Set up an altar in the center of the space in which you are working. Put the candle, salt, incense, water, and the object you chose over it.

II. Cast a circle wide enough for you and the altar.

III. Take some salt and throw it on the object while saying:

> [Insert the name of the object], I exorcise you and purify you.

IV. Hold the object in your hand, take the incense, and go to the east. Say:

> [Insert the name of the object], I awaken you now. By the powers of the air, you now live.

Pass the object through the incense smoke.

V. Light the candle, take it, and go to the south. Say:

> [Insert the name of the object], I awaken you now. By the powers of fire, you now live.

Quickly pass the object through the flame.

VI. Take the water and go to the west. Say:

> [Insert the name of the object], I awaken you now. By the powers of water, you now live.

Sprinkle some water on the object.

VII. Take the salt and go to the north. Say:

> [Insert the name of the object], I awaken you now. By the powers of the earth, you now live.

Throw some salt on it.

VIII. Return to the center and hold the object with your two hands. Look at it and say:

> [Insert the name of the object], you now live, and you are an amulet created to absorb all negative energy, black magic, and curse cast on me. Cleanse my body of all these unclean things. Then you must turn all this negativity into pure and harmless energy. Go now, and do your job.

Keep the amulet for a maximum of 30 days.

## 16 Breaking and Cleansing Spells

**Destroying the amulet**

When you feel you are not under any spell anymore, you must destroy it. Important: even though you think it didn't work, you must destroy it. Don't be arrogant. You must say to the creature that its job is done.

I. Go to the same place where you created the amulet.

II. Perform the same banishing used to create it.

III. Set up the altar and cast a circle.

IV. Take some salt and throw it on the object while saying:

*Creature of amulets, I exorcise you and purify you.*

V. Take some more salt and go to the north. While looking at the object say:

*Amulet, you completed your task; your work is done. I now revoke your creation. You don't exist anymore. By the powers of the earth, you don't live.*

Again, throw some salt on it.

VI. Take the water and go to the west. Say:

*Amulet, you completed your task; your work is done. I now revoke your creation. You don't exist anymore. By the powers of water, you don't live.*

Sprinkle some water on the object.

VII. Light the candle, take it, and go to the south. Say:

*Amulet, you completed your task; your work is done. I now revoke your creation. You don't exist anymore. By the powers of fire, you don't live.*

Quickly pass the object through the flame.

VIII. Take the incense and go to the east. Say:

*Amulet, you completed your task; your work is done. I now revoke your creation. You don't exist anymore. By the powers of the air, you don't live.*

Pass it through the incense smoke.

IX. Close the circle and perform the Banishing Ritual of the Pentagram (see how in the next subject).

X. Throw the object in a river, sea, or bury it deep in the earth.

# Ritual of the Pentagram

Created by the Hermetic Order of the Golden Dawn, this is a powerful ritual designed to banish any chaotic energy from your life and from the space in which you are working. It is widely used to open any magical ceremonies in order to banish all spirits that may be around and have the place cleansed to receive the forces we desire to work with. It can also protect you when it is practiced daily[4], strengthening your aura and making your energy field more balanced and stronger against any spirit with malicious intent or black magic spells.

Aleister Crowley, the most successful magician of the 20th century, writes in his notes on the Ritual of the Pentagram:

> *"Every man has a natural fortress within himself, the soul impregnable. Besides this central citadel, man also has an external fortress, the aura. It is the duty of every person to see that his aura is in good condition. There are two main methods for doing this. The first is by a performance two or three times daily of the Banishing Ritual of the Pentagram. Its main point is to establish in the astral four pentagrams, one in each quarter, and two hexagrams, one above, the other below, thus enclosing the magician, as it were, in a consecrated box. It also places in his aura the divine names invoked."*

## Training Your Visualization

The downside of this ritual for beginners is its visualization process. You must visualize a lot of things, such as spheres of light, pentagrams, circles, crosses, etc. This is really important because all this is actually taking place on the astral plane. For example, if you are drawing a pentagram in the air, you must clearly visualize this pentagram in the air. You can do this with your eyes open or closed. I prefer to stay with my eyes closed because, at least for me, it eases the process. The visualization of colors is also a problem. The standard is to visualize the spheres in brilliant white light, and this can be easy or difficult for you. For me, I find white light a little bit hard to visualize. I prefer other colors like yellow or blue.

To develop your ability to visualize anything with your mind's eye, you need to practice it. Sit down or stand in a quiet place, close your eyes, and begin to imagine things around you, such as spheres of light and pentagrams. Draw anything you want in the air with your index finger and clearly visualize it. Try to keep your drawings active in your mind for as long as possible and don't lose focus. Another exercise you can do is to look at a picture for about three minutes, close your eyes, and try to reproduce it in your mind with all the details. Doing this on a daily basis, you will considerably improve your ability to see with your mind's eye.

## Step by Step

### The Qabalistic Cross

All the spheres of light in this ritual are formed from the same source of light. Other versions of it ask us to imagine those spheres without mentioning where their energy is coming from. I consider it a mistake, and that is why I created a modified version of the Qabalistic Cross.

I. Go to the east and face east. Stand with feet together and arms close to the body. Imagine that a sphere of brilliant white light is descending far from above your head. This sphere is about 10 inches or 25 centimeters in diameter, and now it is right just above your head.

II. With a dagger, wand, or your right index finger, touch the light and bring a fraction of it to the forehead. This smaller sphere is half the size of the one above your head. Touch the forehead and vibrate ATAH.

III. Touch the light again, but this time, point towards your feet and imagine the sphere of light descending to the ground. Vibrate MALKUTH.

IV. Now bring another sphere of light to the right shoulder. Touch the shoulder and vibrate VE-GEBURAH.

V. Bring another sphere to the left shoulder. Touch the shoulder and vibrate VE-GEDULAH.

VI. Put your hands together in front of your chest and vibrate LE-OLAHM. Now clearly imagine the four spheres of light forming a cross and this cross entering your body, filling it with pure light.

VII. Still with hands together vibrate AMEN.

**Drawing the pentagrams**

To trace the pentagrams in the air, you can use a dagger, a wand, or your index finger, preferably the right one. In this tutorial, we are going to work with the index finger.

I. In the east, facing east, draw in the air the Banishing Pentagram of Earth and then bring the point of your finger to its center. Vibrate[5] the name YHVH.

## 20  Breaking and Cleansing Spells

**Figure 2. The Banishing Pentagram of Earth**

The arrow indicates the direction you must draw the pentagram.

II. Without moving your finger in any other direction, start tracing a circle while you move to the south. In the south, trace the Banishing Pentagram of Earth again. Bring your finger to the center and vibrate ADNI.

III. Continue the semi-circle to the west and again trace the pentagram bringing your finger to its center. Vibrate AHIH.

IV. Repeat the same process in the north. Vibrate the name AGLA ATAH GIBOR LE-OLAHM.

V. Now complete the circle bringing your finger again to the center of the pentagram you drew in the east.

VI. Now in the east, stay in cross position (feet together and arms extended) and say:

> Before me, the great Archangel RAPHAEL (vibrate).
>
> Behind me, the great Archangel GABRIEL (vibrate).
>
> At my right hand, the great Archangel MICHAEL (vibrate).
>
> At my left hand, the great Archangel AURIEL (vibrate).

VII. Now say:

> About me, flame the pentagrams.

Imagine the circle and the pentagrams in white flames.

*And in the column shines the six-rayed star.*

Imagine two hexagrams, one under and one above you, shining and forming a grid of light around your body.

VIII. Repeat the Qabalistic Cross, and it is done.

## Pronunciation Guide

Learn how to pronounce the words and names used in this ritual as they are pronounced in Hebrew.

Table 1. Pronunciation guide

| | |
|---|---|
| ATAH (You are) | ah-tah |
| MALKUTH (the Kingdom) | mah-hoot |
| VE-GEBURAH (and Power) | veh-geh-boo-rah[6] |
| VE-GEDULAH (and Glory) | veh-geh-doo-lah |
| LE-OLAHM (forever) | leh-olahm |
| YHVH | ye-hoh-vah |
| ADNI | ah-doh-nye |
| AHIH | eh-heh-yeh |
| AGLA | ah-gah-lah |
| GIBOR | gee-bor[7] |
| RAPHAEL | rah-fah-el |
| GABRIEL | gah-vree-el |
| MICHAEL | mee-hah-el |
| AURIEL | au-hee-el |

The above pronunciations and the ones found in the Appendix of this book were transcribed after listening many times to audios of native Hebrew speakers. I did the best I could, but unfortunately, English has some limitations when we try to transcribe sounds from other languages.

## Endnotes

1. This is a phrase taken from the ancient Eleusinian Mysteries that means "far, far from this place, be the profane."
2. If you don't know how to pass your hands through the flame of a candle without getting burn, please don't do this.
3. This means pronouncing a word aloud, vibrating the syllables.
4. In order to practice the Banishing Ritual of the Pentagram on a daily basis, you also need to practice the Invoking Ritual of the Pentagram (see the Appendix). Otherwise, your energy will be unbalanced.
5. All the four names of God in this ritual must be intensely vibrated to the limits of the universe.
6. The "e" in "veh" and "geh" sounds pretty similar to the one in "eight." And the "g" in "geh" sounds like the one in "guide."
7. The "g" in "gee" sounds like the one in "guide."

# CHAPTER 3

# LOVE SPELLS

There is a big chance you are reading this book mainly because of this chapter. You may be hungry to know how to cast some spells to bring back the love of your life, and I promise you will know it, but first, I must say there is no such thing as a love spell. Love is the most beautiful feeling a human can have, and it happens naturally. Love spells are about forcing someone to like you and changing someone's life. This is not love but persuasion and manipulation. And this is why love spells belong to the category of black magic. When you change someone's life for your benefit or the benefit of others without his or her consent, you are doing black magic. You may be thinking, what is the problem? Well, if you believe in karma, there is a big problem: you are bringing bad karma to you because we can't mess with someone's life without paying for that. In case you don't care about it, you are good to go. Decide for yourself if you should or should not cast this kind of spell.

# Love Spell 01

This spell will make the person you love think about you all the time.

## Things You Will Need

- An apple.
- A rose flower.
- A red paper heart with the name, date of birth, and zodiac sign of the beloved person written on it.
- A red paper heart with your name, date of birth, and zodiac sign written on it.
- Seven wooden toothpicks.
- A glass of water with three teaspoons of salt.
- A clean knife.

## Step by Step

**Banishing**

I. Place your hand above the glass of water and say:

*Creature of water, I consecrate you and awaken you immediately. I purify the essence of this fluid so that it can expel and remove all negativity, and bless everything it touches.*

II. Sprinkle the space in which you are purifying with the consecrated water while saying:

*I invite all harmful forces to leave right now. By the creature of water, may this place be blessed and I purified. I now proclaim the sacred silence.*

III. Stay in silence for a moment visualizing the place being cleansed. Concentrate on a violet flame cleansing and taking away all negative energy.

IV. When you feel ready and purified, start the ceremony.

**The ritual**

I. Sprinkle some of the holy water on the paper heart with the name of the beloved person written on it. Hold the paper and focus entirely on the person in question and say:

> *Creature of paper, I consecrate you, so that you represent [insert the name of the person]. You are [insert the name of the person] in body, soul, and spirit. You are the head and mind of [insert the name of the person]. You are a connection with [insert the name of the person], and you are the key to the heart of [insert the name of the person], born on [insert the date of birth of the person].*

II. Stay focused until you feel you have created a connection with your target.

III. When you feel the connection was created, hold the apple and say:

> *Fruit of lust, fruit of passion, fruit of seduction, and temptation, now send your powers and your energy to my rite.*

IV. Concentrate on passion and lust, thinking about the person and bringing this feeling into you.

V. Hold the rose flower and say:

> *Mystical flower of the holy mysteries, flower of love and power. Remember now the ancestral knowledge and send your sensuality and your love. Rose, I invoke your love mysteries.*

VI. Think about what you want and begin to visualize your desire, repeating it until you are tired and feeling a powerful energy in you. This takes from 10 to 20 minutes.

VII. Take the paper heart with your name written on it, sprinkle some water, and say:

> *Creature of paper, I consecrate you, so that you represent me, I [insert your name] in body, soul, and spirit. You are my head and my mind, you are a connection with me, and so receive my energy.*

VIII. Put a drop of saliva on this same paper. Ideally, you should put a drop of blood, but saliva will work as well.

IX. Then, using a clean knife, cut the apple in half vertically and remove the seeds which will be used at the end of this ritual. Place the paper with the name of the person you love on one part of the apple and the paper with your name over it so that the names are facing each other.

X. Rejoin the two halves of the apple and start sticking the toothpicks while saying:

> *May love, friendship, and fellowship flourish between the heart of [insert the name of the person] and my heart. So that together, I [insert your name] and [insert the name of the person] can share the purest love, the love that keeps the flame of life alive, powerful love, glorious, heavenly, and dreamy.*

XI. With the last toothpick, stick the rose flower on the top of the apple. Raise the apple and raise the energy, thinking about your goal.

XII. Keep the apple seeds in a little bag for as long as you think is necessary.

XIII. Dispose of the apple in the woods or somewhere else surrounded by trees.

# Love Spell 02: Working with Lilith

## Everything About Lilith

Most of the things one can find about Lilith on the internet or other magic books are incomplete or wrong. Some describe her as Adam's first wife, a demon, a sex goddess, etc. No one seems to agree on what she really is, and, to be frank, we don't need to, as I am going to show in the next paragraph. The descriptions of her powers and what she can do for those who ask her for help are also limited, considering she is a spirit with so much potential but unknown to most of the occultists. So, before proceeding to the actual work, I am going to show what Lilith is and what you can get from her.

Lilith, Laylah, Darkat, Layil is the embodiment of the night. She has black hair, red eyes, and the animals that represent her are the snake, the dog, and the bull. She likes apple, peach, white lilies, red roses, red wine, pure water, attar of roses. She is the angel of prostitution of Zoroastrian Kabbalah, being the mother of seduction, illusion, abortion, freedom, and prostitutes. She is a sorceress and works hard on sexual matters, passions, dreams, and vampirism. For paganism, she is a moon goddess, and in orthodox Judaism, she is a part of Shekinah (feminine presence or manifestation of the Jewish God). In modernity, she went through many changes and became the feminine side of Satan. She is everything that came before the Jewish God and everything that opposes him; that is, she is good and bad at the same time. She can do anything, but her specialty is witchcraft and sexuality. For her, always white or red candles. She is the mistress of dreams, and through dreams and sex, she sucks the vital energy of people, which is the energy present in semen or blood, the energy of one's life. There is no need to classify her as a god, angel, or demon because she is an ancient and powerful spirit, and that is enough for us to show her all due respect.

She, like all the other spirits, has two sides that one may define as evil and good, which I don't agree with. The definition of what is evil and what is good is so human and simplistic that it can't be completely applied to the astral plane. The evil side of Lilith is mainly credited to her mother of abortion personality and because sometimes she may not like being evoked, and so she may be a little rude, especially if you have nothing that interests her. But since we are not going to actually evoke Lilith in our spell and we are not going to ask her anything related to babies or kids, everything should run smoothly in our operation.

## Things You Will Need

- A saucer.
- A red or white candle.
- Two strawberries or apples.
- A red paper or plush heart with the name of the beloved person written behind it.
- The seal of Lilith.
- Sterilized needle (optional).

## Step by Step

### Banishing

Say:

*In the name of Layil, mistress of the night, of wrath and storms, I command all negativity to leave this place. By the power of Layil, mistress of destruction and punishment, I send back everything thrown at me, and I break the obstacles that prevent my magic.*

PROCUL, O PROCUL ESTE PROFANI. *Profane and unclean spirits go away.*

**The ritual**

I. Arrangements

Everything used in this spell you put on the saucer. The strawberries or apples are used to decorate it. Arrange everything in a way that pleases you. Put the seal of Lilith in front of the saucer.

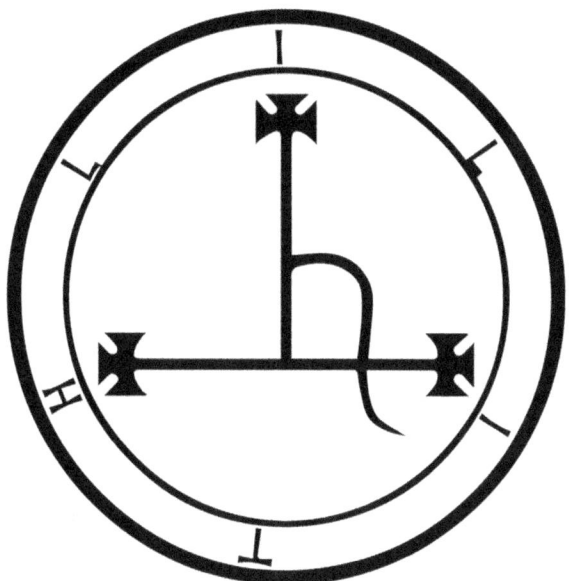

**Figure 3. The seal of Lilith**

II. Invocation

*Lilith, holy angel of prostitution, hear me.*

*I invoke you, mother of rebellion and seduction.*

*Look at me now with your red eyes.*

*Ignite me with the fire of desires and with your lust.*

*Drown me in the lakes of passion.*

*Put in my hands the apple of desire, the pear of sweetness, and the peach of lust.*

*Now build the carpet of lilies for my walk.*

*Put in my body the aroma of the rose, the burning of the pepper, and in my lips the honey.*

*Open the doors of your world to me; bring me joy and achievements.*

*Give me the treasures of this land and let me be the temptation.*

*Hail Laylah.*

## The sacred act of masturbation

First, I need to point out that masturbation, when used in rituals, is considered a holy act. Bear in mind that you are not masturbating to have fun but to release the necessary energy for the spell to work.

III. Focus on Lilith for a few minutes and vibrate her name.

IV. Begin the sacred act (masturbation) with the left hand visualizing your desire and keeping in mind that it is coming true. Hold your orgasm as long as you can, and when you cannot, ejaculate and put in your mouth the elixir of life (semen). Spit it on the candle and spread it, "masturbate" the candle while strongly visualizing your desires, and when you feel a force inside of you wanting to leave, you light the candle, as if it had ejaculated and was sending the energy to your goal.

V. Say:

*In the name of Lilith, the spell begins.*

*By the power of Lilith, [insert the name of the person] is mine.*

*I now change your mind.*

*Just as my heart is yours, so is my desire.*

*You love me; you are attracted to me. In me, is your passion and your heart.*

VI. Pierce your finger and drip three drops of blood on the heart. (optional)

VII. Then hold the heart and think as if you were the person you love:

*I love [insert your name].*

*I want you, I desire you, I need you.*

*You are the reason I wake up every day.*

*Our love is greater than ourselves.*

*Our love is what makes us one.*

*My heart I give to you, and forever, we shall be together.*

VIII. Let the candle burn to the end in a place without risk of fire. Keep the heart with you or bury it, preferably in the woods.

Note: this spell is ideal for men because of the masturbation part. If you are a woman, you can also perform the sacred act of masturbation, but you will not be able to use the elixir of life that only men possess. You can use a drop of blood to replace the semen and give energy to the spell. It will work in the same way.

# Love Spell 03: Working with Baal

## Everything About Baal

Baal is an ancient god who was worshiped by the Canaanites and Phoenicians. His name means Lord. In the Goetia, he is considered a powerful king who governs in the east and has legions of spirits under his command. Baal Hadad is the god of storm, rain, fertility, abundance, and ruler of the world. To work with him, one must offer him water representing harmony, balance, and destruction; salt representing plenty or death; fruits, grains, and wine. To get in touch with Baal, it is necessary to have a representation of him that can be a physical or mental image, in addition to a prayer. You must be patient when working with this god, and worshiping him with daily prayers and offerings is the best way to get his attention. Baal is such a versatile god that this same spell can be used for other purposes.

## Things You Will Need

- A glass of water.
- Fruits and grains.

## Step by Step

### Purification

I. Raise the glass of water and say:

> In the name of Baal Hadad, Lord of Order and Rain, I consecrate the essence of this fluid to purify everything it touches.

II. Sprinkle the space with the water and drink some of it.

### The ritual

I. Opening

> I come forth to perform this sacred act. It is my wish to connect with Baal and with the holy Elohim. I greet the gods of the past; I salute the gods of Canaan, the land of prosperity and happiness.

*Hail El, the father of mankind. Hail El Elyon. Abu, Abu Adami; Abu, Abu Shanima (in the Canaanite language, it means Father, Father of Man; Father, Father of Time).*

II. Think of Baal, in his aspects, focus on him, and invoke:

*I invoke the sacred name of Baal Shamem, the Lord of Heaven and Thunder.*

*Baal son of El, Baal Aliyan, the one who prevails.*

*Baal Lord of Justice and Grains, Baal Son of Dagon, Baal Zephon, Lord of the North, Baal Anthar, Baal Brathy, Baal Karmelos, Baal Marqo, Baal Gad, Baal Hammom, and all the other names that you may want to be called, I invoke you.*

*Baal Reginon, Lord of Raven and Thunder, Lord of Destruction, come to me.*

*Baal Hadad, Lord of Rain and Fertility.*

*Hail Baal, who defeats Mot and Yam.*

III. Offer fruits and grains to Baal.

IV. Prayer

*Baal, Mighty and Powerful God, I come before you to humbly ask for your help.*

*I am in love with someone who is not in love with me, and I wish to change that.*

*May your powers make [insert the name of the person you love] loves me the way I love him (her).*

*May your powers make [insert the name of the person you love] desires me the way I desire him (her).*

*Because I know Lord Baal, from now on, he (she) can't live without me.*

*His (her) mind is now changed, and there is love between us.*

*Hail Baal Hadad. Amen.*

V. Meditation

*Baal, Mighty Lord, you who have turned away from humanity because of blasphemy, come to me. I call you with a holy and reverent mind.*

VI. Silence your mind and your thoughts, focusing on Baal. Keep silent as if you were waiting for something.

# Love Spell 04: Working with Aphrodite

This spell is not to bring someone you love, it will bring someone that will love you into your life, and this is completely different from the other love spells we learned so far. Here we have a case of white magic because you will not mess with anyone's life but will just ask for your true love to come into your life. So, we can conclude there is no karma involved here, in case you believe it.

## Brief Note on Aphrodite

Aphrodite is a goddess of Greek mythology, also worshiped by the Romans. She is the daughter of Zeus and Dione, and her Roman equivalent is the Goddess Venus. She is the goddess of beauty, fertility, love, and sexuality.

## Things You Will Need

- An apple.
- Seven strawberries.
- Seven red rose petals.
- Seven cloves.

- Honey.
- A red candle.
- A white candle.
- A white bowl.
- A glass of water.

This ritual should take place on Friday, the day of Venus.

## Step by Step

**Purification**

I. First, you need to purify yourself physically and spiritually. Take a bath to cleanse your body, and wear clean clothes. Meditate and clear your mind of all unholy thoughts. If it is possible for you and if you want to, you can go without eating meat for 24 hours before the ritual.

II. Start the purification by saying the Homeric Hymn 23 to the Son of Cronus:

> I will sing of Zeus, chiefest among the gods and greatest, all-seeing, the lord of all, the fulfiller who whispers words of wisdom to Themis as she sits leaning towards him. Be gracious, all-seeing Son of Cronos, most excellent and great.

III. Then say:

> Hekas hekas este bebeloi. Far, far from this place, be the profane.

IV. Place your hand above the glass of water and say:

> Creature of water, in the name of Zeus, Son of Cronus, I purify you.

V. Sprinkle the space in which you are purifying with the consecrated water while saying:

> O theoi genoisthe apotropoi kakon. May the gods turn away evils.

## The ritual

I. Light the white candle and say the Homeric Hymn 10 to Aphrodite:

> *Of Cythera, born in Cyprus, I will sing. She gives kindly gifts to men; smiles are ever on her lovely face, and lovely is the brightness that plays over it. Hail, goddess, queen of well-built Salamis and sea-girt Cyprus; grant me a cheerful song. And now I will remember you and another song also.*

II. Proceed to the invocation:

> *Aphrodite, goddess of love, I invoke you.*
>
> *Daughter of Zeus, goddess of pleasure, goddess of beauty, goddess of sexuality, I invoke you.*
>
> *I beg for your help with the mysteries of love and sex.*
>
> *Throw your ancient mysteries at me.*
>
> *Open the gates of love and pleasure in my life.*
>
> *Bring me love and make me beautiful and attractive.*
>
> *No man (woman) will look at me without desire, but among them, a special one will come to me.*
>
> *He (she) is the one who loves me.*
>
> *Hail Aphrodite, goddess of many virtues.*

III. Put the rose petals and the cloves in the bowl, and say:

> *In the name of Aphrodite, I will be beautiful and attractive.*

IV. Put the strawberries and apple, and say:

> *In the name of Aphrodite, I will have pleasure in my life.*

V. Cover everything with honey and say:

> *In the name of Aphrodite, love will come into my life.*

VI. Light the red candle and say:

*So mote it be.*

VII. Bury the contents of the bowl in the woods or somewhere else surrounded by trees.

# CHAPTER 4

# BEAUTY SPELLS

This type of spell I could easily have included in the previous chapter since your problems with love may be only a matter of lack of confidence in yourself, and the proper gods can help you to achieve that and even the beauty pattern you think you don't have. But maybe your problems are not related to love, and you just want to feel beautiful, to change the person you think you are, to look at the mirror and see something that pleases you, and to be praised by others for your physical characteristics. So, if this is your case, the spells in this chapter will certainly help you with that.

Beauty spells work, both changing your perception of yourself and your body shape as well. The first effect of these spells is to make the person who cast it to accept the fact that they are beautiful indeed. When you change your perception of yourself, people will also start looking at you in a different way. The other effect you can expect are physical changes in your body, and this can happen in many scales from soft to a complete disappearance of the unwanted characteristic. What one must bear in mind is that depending on the problem, significant changes can't occur physically. Supposing a small person wants to grow little inches more, but they are not in the growth stage anymore, the desired effect is unlikely to happen. The same goes for someone with a big nose where little differences can be noticed, but it will not have a considerable reduction. On the other hand, other problems like spots, scars, wrinkles, hair, etc., can be completely resolved.

## Frey and Freya

Frey is a Norse god, King of the Vanir, god of prosperity, harvest, mysteries, virility, and fertility. Frey is Freya's brother, goddess of beauty, love, sensuality, magic, and protective goddess of pregnant women. Frey and Freya bring together all the characteristics that the word beauty carries. They are powerful gods always willing to help those who invoke them because, like most gods, they have been forgotten by mankind.

**Figure 4. Frey**

42  Beauty Spells

**Figure 5. Freya**

## Things You Will Need

➢ A red or white candle.

➢ A glass of water, wine, or mead.

➢ A little plate.

➢ An image of Freya (you can use the Figure 5 of this book or search on Google for one that pleases you better).

➢ Some seeds or grains.

# Step by Step

**Pre-ritual**

I. Take a bath to purify your body.

II. Say out loud:

*Bearer of the mighty hammer Mjölnir.*

*Hail Thor Veu.*

III. Go to the north, make the hammer sign, and say:

*Hammer of Thor, protects us in the northern paths. All suffering must go away.*

The hammer sign:

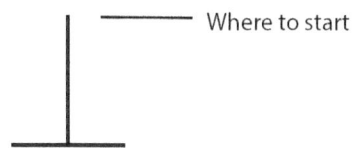

**Figure 6. The hammer sign**

IV. Go to the east, make the hammer sign, and say:

*Hammer of Thor, protects us in the eastern paths. All suffering must go away.*

V. Repeat the same process in the south and west.

VI. Return to the north, looking at the sky, make the hammer sign, and say:

*Hammer of Thor, give us the blessing of the heavens.*

VII. Looking at the ground, make the hammer sign, and say:

*Hammer of Thor, give us the blessing of the womb of the Earth.*

VIII. Stay in the Algiz position.

Algiz position: stand with your arms extended above your head, forming a 90-degree angle between them. Feel that your body is like a tree, visualizing the trunk and the crown, and feeling the force flowing through you, revering the sacredness of your body while vibrating the name ALGIZ.

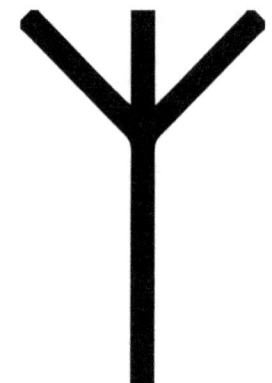

**Figure 7. The Algiz position**

Algiz is one of the most powerful runes; it illustrates a horned animal, a tree, and a man with the arms stretched out. Algiz describes the search and contact with the higher powers, and how to receive their protection. The Algiz rune can be seen as the awakening of sexual forces and how they can activate the warrior spirit. In divination, this rune can be interpreted as the awakening of inner forces and the effort to attain divinity.

**The ritual**

I. Place your hands above the altar and say:

> *I bless and make this altar a sacred place for the service of Freya, banishing all profane and impure influences. May my mind, in this blessed place, also be blessed. As Heimdall guards the Bifrost bridge, may this place be guarded against all forces that oppose my rite today.*

II. Meditate with Freya for some minutes. Stay in the Algiz position and invoke:

> *Frú Freya (frú = frau = lady), goddess of pleasures and sensuality, goddess of love and fertility, wealth, and earthly pleasures. We know you, mistress of life, in the*

*field in fertile beasts, but also in the wombs of women. Goddess of pleasures and affection, I greet you for the many delights in Midgard. I thank you for life, for fertility, and when the dead warriors fall on battlefields, you gather the heroes and take them to your hall of pleasures. Come, Freya, in the form of a cat.*

*Falcon feathers woman, lady of the Seidr. I invoke you lady who cries tears of gold; witch, warrior, bearer of the Brisingamen.*

*Hail Freya.*

III. Focus on Freya for one minute and say:

*Goddess of love and lust, welcome.*

*Daughter of Niord, welcome.*

*Sister of Lord Frey, welcome.*

*Goddess of the Vanir, welcome.*

*Wife of Od, welcome.*

*Lady of magic, welcome.*

*Lady of the Valkyries, welcome.*

*Lady of desire, welcome.*

*Lady of wealth, welcome.*

*Lady of beauty, be welcome.*

IV. Relax your body and mind focusing on the image of Freya. Take a deep breath and relax more and more, mentally calling for Freya until you feel a force moving your consciousness. Then say:

*Come to me, Vanadis, to receive this sacrifice prepared for you. Do not take your gifts from me, but continue to send them into my life, in the prosperity and rejoicing* of sensuality in all things. May through this sincere and simple ceremony, I can dry the golden tears of your face. Most beautiful goddess, I invoke you.

V. Raise the glass of water and say:

And I offer you a sacrifice. Not in blood, but the grace of my human efforts, my struggle, and my devotion. May the covenant between man and gods be strong in our fight to defend Asgard or against those who wish to enslave the friends of the gods in Midgard.

VI. Pour a little of the liquid into the dish and say:

Freya, accept this gift, not from a slave or a servant because I have no master. Not as a form of appeasement because everything is fine between us, but as a sign of our communion and likeness.

Show Freya the other offerings at the altar. If it is a liquid, pour it into the same dish. Light the candle offering its flame to Freya and say:

Freya, you received my sacrifice, symbolized by the offerings. Now send your blessings and powers to me so that I can grow and fulfill my desires now. Share your gifts with me.

Hail Freya.

VII. Invoking Frey

King of the Vanir.

Frey, god of the grains.

Warrior without weapon who gave your sword for love.

Yngvi, you make the grains flow in the spring.

God of male beauty, virility, and splendor.

Lord of the light elves.

*Lord of happiness and fertility.*

*I salute you, son of Niord, Freya's brother.*

VIII. Put some of the seeds or grains on the plate, and pour a little more of the liquid saying:

*Lord Frey, accept my sacrifice.*

IX. Relax, focus on Frey and Freya, and say:

*Hail, Hail to the mystery.*

*Frey, Freya, gods of mysteries.*

*King and Queen of the Vanir.*

*Gods of beauty, gods of wealth.*

*Goddess of love and passion.*

*Goddess of sensuality, magic, battle, and seduction.*

*God of the fertile fields, beauty, and virility.*

*God of splendor, happiness, and fertility.*

*Now grant the necessary power to my magic.*

*Bring me the visions, awaken the intuition, and show me what I cannot see.*

*If I dream about verses, bring me the songs, lend me your power.*

*I now desire to obtain sensuality and beauty, the gifts of your nature.*

X. Begin to visualize the type of beauty you want to have, the imperfections of the skin fading, the shape of the face, body. Imagine a red energy filling your body and shaping you. This energy brings you a sweet and feminine beauty, a feminine sensuality, a masculine beauty and virility at the same time. Also, visualize this aura attracting passion, friendships,

## 48 Beauty Spells

affection, powers to seduce, to enchant. When you feel this intense energy inside you, describe with your words what that beauty is for you.

XI. Visualize Freya and Frey, giving you the powers of sensuality, beauty, love, fertility.

*Lofna, in the name of Frey and Freya, send your blessings: betrayal, passion, and homosexuality.*

*Gersemi and Hnoss, in the name of Frey and Freya, send your blessings: love, beauty, and maternity.*

XII. Visualize the desired aspects again, but this time more strongly and fixed on you, as if they went from your interior to your exterior.

XIII. Take a deep breath pulling the energy of Frey and Freya into you; feel the vital energy in your blood as it strengthens your magic; visualize yourself with lovers, men, women, friends, prosperity.

XIV. Relax and empty your mind, and masturbate (only if you are a man) while repeating:

*Freya, bride of the Vanir.*

*Bring love to my heart.*

*Bring me the gifts of beauty.*

*Bring me the gifts of passion.*

*Bring me the gifts of wealth.*

*Oh, Freya, bring me the gifts of your nature.*

*Frey, bring me your power; grant me beauty, love, and pleasure.*

*Bring happiness, peace, and prosperity to my life.*

XV. When you cum, say:

*To Frey and Freya.*

XVI. Mix the semen with saliva and offer to the gods saying:

*Accept this fertile offering.*

XVII. Relax again, focus on Frey and Freya, clear your mind, and meditate some time with them. When you finish, thank them and end the ritual.

*I thank you, Freya, Mighty Goddess of Asgard.*

*Goddess of many names and virtues.*

*I thank you, Frey, Mighty God of Asgard.*

*God of many names and virtues.*

*May there always be peace between us.*

*I do not say goodbye but see you soon.*

*Hail Frey and Freya.*

Note: if you are a woman, skip the masturbation part and go straight to the prayer and final thanks.

# Aphrodite

You can see a description of Aphrodite in Chapter 3.

## Things You Will Need

- Two red candles.
- A bottle of red wine.
- A wine glass (or water glass).
- Rose petals.

- ➢ A glass of water.
- ➢ A white bowl.
- ➢ Rose incense.
- ➢ A mirror bigger enough for you see your body, not necessarily the whole body at once but at least half of it.
- ➢ Ancient Greek music.

## Step by Step

**Purification**

I. First, you need to purify yourself physically and spiritually. Take a bath to cleanse your body, and wear clean clothes. Meditate and clear your mind of all unholy thoughts. If it is possible for you and if you want to, you can go without eating meat for 24 hours before the ritual.

II. To purify the space, say:

*Hekas hekas este bebeloi. Far, far from this place, be the profane.*

III. Place your hand above the glass of water and say:

*Creature of water, I consecrate you and awaken you immediately.*

*I purify the essence of this fluid so that it can expel and remove all negativity, and bless everything it touches.*

IV. Sprinkle the space in which you are purifying with the consecrated water while saying:

*I invite all harmful forces to leave right now. By the creature of water, may this place be blessed and I purified. I now proclaim the sacred silence.*

V. Stay in silence for a moment visualizing the place being cleansed. Concentrate on a violet flame purifying and taking away all negative energy.

**The ritual**

I. In the center of the space in which you are working, put the bowl on the floor with a candle on each side. The incense should be behind it and all the other items in front of the bowl.

II. Burn the incense, light the candles, and call for Aphrodite seven times:

*Aphrodite. Aphrodite. Aphrodite. Aphrodite. Aphrodite. Aphrodite. Aphrodite.*

III. Continue:

*Aphrodite, goddess of love, hear me.*

*Daughter of Zeus, goddess of pleasure, goddess of beauty, goddess of sexuality, I invoke you.*

*Goddess of beauty, share your secrets with me.*

*Show me how I can become beautiful to my eyes and everyone's eyes.*

IV. Pour some wine into the wine glass, raise it, and say:

*Accept this wine as my sacrifice. I give it to you with sincerity and love, but knowing you deserve more and more.*

*Send me your energy and shape my body the way I want it to be.*

*Goddess of beauty and love, make me the most beautiful human being that ever existed.*

V. Raise the glass of water and say:

*This is the elixir of life and beauty.*

*Without it, no man can survive, and no beauty lasts.*

Then pour all the water into the bowl.

VI. Take the rose petals in your hands and say:

*These are the perfect natural representation of beauty.*

VII. Put the petals in the bowl and continue:

*I now ask you, O Great Aphrodite, to send forth your energy into this bowl and turn this mixture into a divine liquid capable of healing all the imperfections of my body, including [say all the things you want to change in your body].*

*Now I offer you some music and dance.*

VIII. Play ancient Greek music and dance around the bowl for some minutes.

IX. Take the bowl and say:

*In the name of Aphrodite, I now change my body to the way I want it to be.*

X. Spread the water over your whole body. Visualize all the imperfections fading away. Say out loud what is changing in you.

XI. Now take the mirror, look at you, and see how beautiful you are. Say it with conviction. Don't doubt it.

XII. Closing the temple

*I thank you for your work on this day, Mighty and Beautiful Aphrodite. I now declare this temple closed.*

# CHAPTER 5

# MONEY SPELLS

Money spells are where most people fail to achieve the desired effect. One can cast a spell to attract money every single month and still not get a single cent more than they already have. It happens because of the lack of objectivity; in other words, asking for money requires an existing source from where it will come. If you want to earn more money in your current job, so you must ask for a job promotion. If you want money by gambling, so ask for that and start betting.

The real problem when you don't specify the source where the money will come from is receiving the money in a very undesirable way. Imagine you suffering a car crash and getting compensation from your insurance, do you want that? I bet you don't. Besides, you should make it clear the spell must work without causing harm to anyone. You don't want to get promoted in your job because your coworker died. You should behave like this with every spell you cast, without harming yourself, your family, your friends, or anyone else.

# Working with Bune

Bune, Bime, or Bim is a spirit that can bring money to those who call him. He is a powerful Duke who rules 30 legions of spirits.

## Things You Will Need

- Two white candles.
- Incense (sandalwood).
- The seal of Bune.
- Well-made food prepared by yourself.

## Step by Step

I. Perform the Banishing Ritual of the Pentagram.

II. Set up an altar with the Triangle of the Art, candles, offerings (food), and incense. Consecrate the triangle.

III. Write your intent on the back of the seal of Bune. For example, "I want to get promoted in my job." Put the seal inside the triangle.

# Money Spells

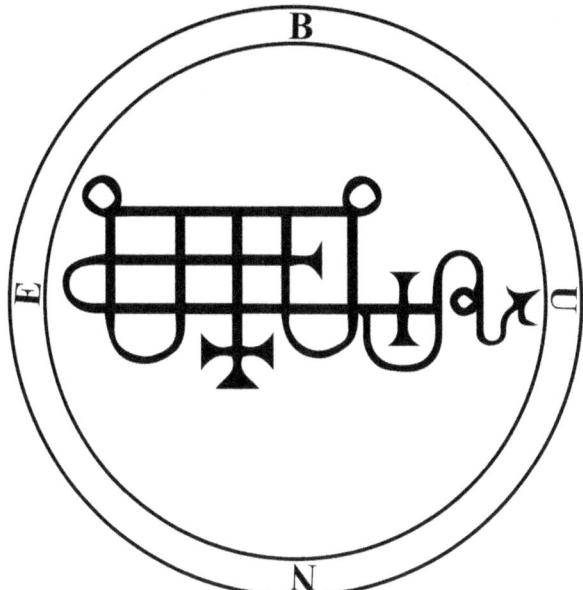

**Figure 8. The seal of Bune**

IV. Light the candles, burn the incense, and cast a circle.

V. Invoking Bune

Recite the following invocation three times:

> *Bune, Bime, Bim, Mighty and Powerful Duke, I invoke you.*
>
> *In the name of the Most High, I call you, and I ask that you receive my requests.*
>
> *Among the many gifts you possess, you master the art of wealth, bringing money to man, quickly and effectively.*
>
> *Come and receive my sacrifice.*

VI. Sacrifice and requests

> *I prepared this food especially for you, as a sign of respect for your great powers.*
>
> *I ask your help with my financial problems.*
>
> *I [insert your name] humbly request that you [insert your wish].*

> Grant my wish within [insert how many days you will give him to fulfill your requests] and without causing harm to myself, my family, my friends, or anyone else.

VII. Thanking Bune

> I thank you, Great Duke Bune, for your presence in this rite.

> You can now go back from where you came from, ready to fulfill what I have asked from you.

VIII. Close the circle and the triangle.

IX. Perform the Banishing Ritual of the Pentagram.

X. You can dispose of the food a few hours later.

XI. Keep the seal until your wish is fulfilled. Then you should deactivate it by saying:

> This seal no longer represents a connection with the spirit Bune. You have no powers anymore.

Then burn it.

If the time you gave the spirit is over and your wish was not fulfilled, deactivate the seal and burn it. You can repeat the spell, but I advise that you try another one.

## Working with Seere

Seere, Sear, or Seir is a mighty prince. He can bring money quickly to those who call him. He rules 26 legions of spirits, and he is often gentle when called. This prince doesn't require great sacrifices or offerings from the magician and will be happy with small things offered to him.

## Things You Will Need

- Two white candles.
- Incense (cedar).
- Well-made food prepared by yourself.

## Step by Step

I. Perform the Banishing Ritual of the Pentagram.

II. Set up an altar with the candles, offerings (food), and incense.

III. Burn the incense, light the candles, and cast a circle.

IV. Invoking Seere

Say the following sentence called ENN thirty times. ENNs are like phone numbers that link you directly to a spirit. Ideally, you should sing it, instead of just speaking it:

> Jeden et Renich Seere tu tasa.

Then, say the following invocation 3x:

> Seere, Sear, Seir, Mighty Prince, I invoke you.
>
> Among the many gifts you possess, you can bring everything quickly, from anywhere in the world, and at any time.
>
> Hear me and come to receive my sacrifice.

V. Sacrifice and requests

> I prepared this food especially for you, as a sign of respect for your great powers.
>
> I ask for your help with my financial problems.
>
> I [insert your name] humbly request that you [insert your wish].

*Grant my wish within [insert how many days you will give him to fulfill your requests] and without causing harm to myself, my family, my friends, or anyone else.*

## VI. Thanking Seere

*I thank you, Prince Seere, for your presence in this rite.*

*You can now go back from where you came from, ready to fulfill what I have asked from you.*

## VII. Close the circle.

## VIII. Perform the Banishing Ritual of the Pentagram.

## IX. You can dispose of the food a few hours later.

Note: it is not the intention of this kind of spell to wait for any manifestation on the part of the spirit. Usually, this work is a one-way communication where only the magician/witch speaks. However, by pronouncing the ENN of Seere 30x as I instructed, Seere may manifest himself somehow, either through the incense smoke and candle flame, or even using the voice.

# CHAPTER 6

# MANIPULATION SPELL

This type of spell is useful when you want to change the mind and control someone's life or make someone take your side. You must already know this is a black magic spell; as previously explained, when you mess with somebody's life, you are doing nothing but black magic, and perhaps there are consequences for those who practice it.

Unlike the previous chapters where were presented two or more spells for each area, in chapter 6, I decided to include only one. This is because manipulation spells require a very powerful spirit that possesses the ability to manipulate people and will agree to do the job for you. When you work with spirits like Bune to get promoted in your job for example, he will have to manipulate your bosses, but this is different because you are not directly asking him to manipulate anyone. So, I can only think of a spirit that has the necessary requisites to perform this task, and he is Belial.

# Working with Belial

Belial is a mighty king who governs 50 legions of spirits. He is believed to have been created right after Lucifer, so you can imagine how ancient and powerful he is. Working with Belial requires patience and confidence since he can completely ignore, manipulate, or deceive you if you think he is not great enough or if you show your weaknesses to him. A pre-ritual where you introduce yourself to Belial through prayers and offerings before calling him is the best way to get his collaboration.

Everyone who works with this spirit agrees on one point: he doesn't like being called a king. He occupies this position, but the best is always refer to him only as Belial.

## Things You Will Need

- Three white candles.
- Incense (frankincense).
- Water, salt, food, objects, etc. Whatever you choose to offer him.
- The seal of Belial.
- Sterilized needle

## Step by Step

**Pre-ritual**

I. Activating the seal of Belial

Hold the seal in your hand and gaze at it for three minutes. Absorb all the details in your mind. Then, say:

*Seal, you now represent a connection with Belial. So mote it be.*

Manipulation Spell 61

**Figure 9. The seal of Belial**

II. Devotion

For three days before casting the spell, recite the following prayer to Belial and offer him a different thing each day:

> *Mighty and Powerful Belial, hear me. I come to you willing to receive your teachings and glory. Accept my sacrifice symbolized by this offering as a sign of our communion and respect.*

Keep silent for a moment. You can dispose of the offering a few hours later.

**The ritual**

I. Perform the Banishing Ritual of the Pentagram.

II. Set up the altar with the Triangle of the Art and incense. Put a candle on each edge of the triangle and consecrate it.

III. Put the seal inside the triangle, burn the incense, and light the candles.

IV. Cast a circle.

## Manipulation Spell

V. Invoke (3x):

> O Mighty and Powerful Belial, great and feared, I invoke you.
>
> I ask you to listen to me and be willing to receive my requests.
>
> Your powers and abilities are what I need right now.
>
> Wherever you are in the world, I invoke you, Belial.

VI. Sacrifice and requests

> I humbly offer you this [insert the name of what you are offering] and a drop of my blood.
>
> Listen to me and help me to [insert your wish].
>
> Grant my wish within [insert how many days you will give him to fulfill your requests] and without causing harm to myself, my family, my friends, or anyone else.

Use a sterilized needle to pierce your finger and drip a drop of blood on the altar. This is necessary because you are asking Belial to manipulate someone, and this is not something easy to do. Your blood will provide more energy to Belial.

VII. Thanking the spirit

> I thank you, spirit Belial for your help in this rite.
>
> Your presence honors me because I know how powerful you are.
>
> You can now go back from where you came from, ready to fulfill what I have asked from you.

VIII. Close the circle and the triangle.

IX. You can dispose of the offerings a few hours later.

X. Perform the Banishing Ritual of the Pentagram.

# CHAPTER 7

# FINDING ANSWERS

When we want to find answers for questions about the present or the future, we are talking about divination, which is a practice widely used by magicians and witches since it is considered a must-do before any magical operation. When we are preparing to perform an evocation or to cast a spell, we should try to find out what could possibly block our magic, if the entity we intend to call will help us, etc. The problem with divination is due to the complexity of its reliable methods like Tarot and scrying that requires dedication from the magician and at least months of practice.

Before writing this chapter when I was still wondering if I should include a discussion about divination in this book, I had a hard time deciding what reliable and accessible divination method I could teach in just a few pages. It would not be possible to explain how Tarot works because it would take half of a book. Scrying was also out of the question since you don't learn how to scry, that is a gift you are born with. Of course, you can practice scrying and try to develop this skill, but it will not be the same. The pendulum is another divination method that is considerably easy since you just need a small object hanging on a rope, but in my experience, pendulums are not suitable for divination. Most of the time, it gives you accurate answers only for things that your conscious or subconscious mind already knows. If you ask the pendulum questions about the future, you will probably get wrong answers since your subconscious doesn't know the answers yet. But pendulums can be useful if you are not sure about what directions you should take in your life because it can access your subconscious, which is a giant library that never forgets anything.

In this chapter, I present three divination methods that are easy to use and more efficient than a pendulum. First, you will learn how to discover the name of your guardian angel and demon. Once you know their names, you can ask them questions about your life because they know everything about you in the present and future time, and they have no reason to lie to you. The second method uses a simple pack of cards, and the last one is called free writing.

# The Name of Your Guardian Angel and Demon

A guardian angel is an angel that follows you from the first day of your life until the last one. He guides and protects you in all phases of your life, even if you don't know he exists. A guardian demon acts in a similar manner but with less influence in your life since we tend to ignore and repel everything related to demons.

Demons are spirits that can't be called angels because, in a very distant time, they lost that status for some reason that we can't be sure about. But they are not spirits of hell as you may think. A magician must know that hell doesn't exist, and the astral plane is far more complicated than the simple Christian definition of heaven and hell.

Working with demons tends to be easier than working with angels. They come quickly and can better understand our mortal necessities while angels may have some difficulties. This not means you should avoid working with angels at all. They are really powerful creatures with many functions in the universe, and one of them is to help humans. They just need to trust you; in other words, you have to create a bond with them and not just ask for a one-time favor.

## Method 1 – Pendulum

Although the pendulum is not a reliable way of divination, we are going to use it in the process of trying to find the name of your guardian angel or demon because I also provide here an easy way for you to check if the information you got from it is correct.

**Calibrating the pendulum**

If you are a beginner or if you are using a new pendulum, you need to calibrate it first.

I. Hold the pendulum between your thumb and index finger, always allowing it to swing freely. If you want, you can sit down and rest your elbow on a table in front of you.

II. Ask the pendulum "show me a yes," and it moves, showing you which movement means yes. Ask "show me a no" and see which movement means no.

III. Now ask obvious questions like "is my name [your name]?". Only stop asking obvious questions when you get only correct answers.

IV. Now that you have calibrated your pendulum, you need to make a bigger copy of the following table:

Table 2. Pendulum

| 1 | 2 | 3 | 4 | 5 |
|---|---|---|---|---|
| 6 | 7 | 8 | 9 | A |
| B | C | D | E | F |
| G | H | I | J | K |
| L | M | N | O | P |
| Q | R | S | T | U |
| V | W | X | Y | Z |

**Preparation**

I. Choose a quiet place to work.

II. Perform the Banishing Ritual of the Pentagram.

III. Take a pen and blank paper for you to write down the answers.

IV. Cast a circle.

V. Sit down inside the circle and relax for a while. Put the paper with the numbers and letters on the ground in front of you.

VI. Give your pendulum the following instructions:

*Pendulum, you are going to move only over the right numbers and letters.*

**Asking the pendulum**

I. Hold the pendulum and start asking the following questions:

1. *How many letters have the name of my guardian angel/demon?* – Place the pendulum over each number for 5-10 seconds. When it moves, you got your answer.

2. *What is the first letter of my guardian angel's/demon's name?* – Place the pendulum over each letter till you get the right one. Repeat it for the following letters according to the number you got in the first question.

II. After finishing with the questions, close the circle and perform the Banishing Ritual of the Pentagram.

**Checking the information**

I. Go to google.com and search for angel/demon + name, example: demon Aym; angel Haniel.

II. If you find any result related to angels or demons, what you got from the pendulum is correct.

III. In case you could not find anything useful on Google, repeat the search using quotes. Example: "demon Aym"; "angel Haniel."

If even after using quotes, you don't get any results related to angels or demons, it means that either the name of your guardian spirit isn't on the internet or the pendulum didn't work for you. In this case, you have one last option you could try.

IV. Search for names of angels and demons, and study their pattern. Generally, these names share some similarities. Compare them with the names you have. If they have nothing in common, forget it and try using the Ouija Board, our next subject.

# Method 2 - Ouija Board

The Ouija Board, also known as Spirit Board, is a tool used to contact spirits in order to get answers from them. This is also not a recommended method for divination because there is a high probability that when using it, you are, in fact, talking to yourself, or the spirits are lying to you. Another negative point is that we don't know what kind of spirits we are dealing with.

When using the board, a door is automatically open, and any kind of spirit can come through to talk to the practitioner. This is why you should use the board always with someone else to prevent you from being too vulnerable to be deceived by the spirits. Another reason you should not use it alone is to prevent your mind from interfering in the answers. So, follow all the recommendations given below.

Figure 10. Ouija Board

Note: only use the board if the pendulum didn't work for you. Don't use it to check if the information the pendulum gave you is correct.

## Using the board

I. Perform the Banishing Ritual of the Pentagram.

II. Cast a circle wide enough for two people.

III. These two people that we are going to call "operators" must sit down inside the circle with the board in front of them.

IV. The operators place their index fingers on the planchette. Don't put much pressure on it.

V. One of the operators ask:

*Are there any spirits here willing to answer my questions?*

VI. When you get a yes, proceed to the following question:

*Have you ever lived?*

VII. If the answer is yes, go to the section Closing the Board. This is because only spirits of dead people would answer yes to this question, and they have nothing to offer you.

VIII. If the answer is no, ask the next question:

*What is your name?*

IX. If the spirit refuses to give you his name, say:

*I am the ruler of this place. Those who want to participate in this ritual must say their names because this is my rule. Say your name right now or leave.*

X. If the spirit refuses to give his name again, go to the section Closing the Board and try again later. Otherwise, you can continue with the next question.

XI. Show your authority to the spirit:

*I am the governor of this place, and I have established a major rule. You must give only true answers to all my questions. Are you willing to follow this rule?*

XII. If the answer is no, close the board, if it is yes, proceed:

*What is the name of my guardian angel/demon?*

XIII. Write down the name given. Don't ask any more questions. Don't be tempted to ask questions about your personal life.

**Closing the board**

I. Once you got the name of your angel or demon, you must close the door you opened. Start it by saying:

> I thank you for answering my questions, and now I say goodbye.

II. Wait for the planchette to move towards the "goodbye" on the table. Whatever if it moves or not, you must say the following:

> All my questions were answered, and now all the entities present here must leave. In the name of ADONAI, and in my name, the ruler of this place, I declare this temple closed.

III. Turn the board upside down.

IV. Close the circle and perform the Banishing Ritual of the Pentagram.

**Checking the information**

Repeat the same process to verify the information received, used in the pendulum section. If you don't get positive results, I am afraid the board also didn't work for you. Of course, it is possible that the names of your guardian spirits are not on the internet, or their names have nothing in common with the names of other angels and demons, but it is not a good sign.

## Establishing Contact

Once you have the name of your angel or your demon, it is time to contact him. You should work only with one of them at least until you get more experience and decide for yourself it is safe to have two different spirits guiding you.

Make a prayer with your own words, saying you truly want him to reveal himself to you. Recite it every day until you feel his presence more and more. Before the prayer, you should vibrate the name of your guardian angel or demon for about two minutes. You may also try to find his seal on the internet; it would be very helpful. If you find the seal, use it before the prayer, gazing at it while you vibrate his name. Clear your mind and meditate, waiting for any sign from him. He can contact you through almost any means, including dreams, the internet, movies, etc. You could be watching a movie, and suddenly some character says something that grabs your attention and immediately makes you think about your guardian angel or demon; this is a message from him.

Once the contact has been established, you can use a pendulum to ask questions, as long as you feel their presence first because using a pendulum without making sure your angel/demon is with you, will not give you good results. Other ways to receive answers will depend on the bond between you and them. They will show what will work best for you.

# Getting Answers from a Deck of Cards

The cards have powers and can give us answers to almost everything in our lives, showing us the future or, more commonly, the paths we should follow. The Tarot and Gypsy Deck are the two most used methods of divination through cards. The Tarot is more complex and has more than seventy different cards with each card representing a different meaning. Both the Tarot and Gypsy Deck are not suitable for yes or no questions. They can't specifically answer if your boyfriend is cheating on you or if you will marry someday. If you ask them something like this, the chances of you getting even more confused are high. That is why many Tarot readers will not allow their clients to ask specific questions.

A simple deck of cards can be transformed into a magical tool for divination, ideal for everyday questions. You can use it to ask if you should go to a party, if you should call someone, or even if you should or not cast a spell. Unfortunately, like all the other yes or no oracles, questions about the future can't be properly answered. So, avoid asking what you will happen in your life.

## Step by Step

I. Buy a new deck of playing cards.

II. Write YES on the Nine of Hearts and NO on the Nine of Spades.

III. Usually, a deck comes with two Jokers, but you are going to use only one, the other you put aside. The Joker is the MAYBE card.

### Consecrating the deck

The deck must be consecrated to the four elements; otherwise, it will have no powers.

I. You will need incense (any type), a glass of water, a candle, and salt or soil.

II. Go to the place where you consecrate your tools and set up an altar in a space where you can walk around it. Put the deck on the altar.

III. In the area around the altar put the incense in the east, the candle in the south, the glass of water in the west, and the salt in the north.

IV. Go to the west of the altar, face east and open the temple saying:

*I call the highest forces in the universe to guide me in this ritual. The intention of this work is to consecrate and give the necessary powers for this deck of cards to become a magical tool capable of answering everything I ask it.*

V. Go to the east, burn the incense, and say:

*I invoke the guardians of the east, powerful sylphs. Lend me the powers of the air, so I can do what I must do today.*

VI. Go to the south, light the candle, and say:

*I invoke the guardians of the south, powerful salamanders. Lend me the powers of fire so I can do what I must do today.*

VII. Go to the west, take the glass of water, and say:

*I invoke the guardians of the west, powerful undines. Lend me the powers of water so I can do what I must do today.*

VIII. Go to the north and take some salt in your hands. Say:

*I invoke the guardians of the north, powerful gnomes. Lend me the powers of the earth, so I can do what I must do today.*

IX. Take the deck, go to the east, and say:

*May the guardians of the east consecrate and empower this deck of cards.*

Pass the deck through the incense smoke.

Repeat the same action in the south, west, and north. Important: you don't pass the deck through the candle flame. Holding the candle in one hand and the deck in the other while asking the guardians of the south to consecrate it is enough. The same goes for water. Water can damage it, so be careful.

X. After finishing in the north, spread the cards over the altar. Point your wand at the deck and say:

*Deck of cards, you are now magical. By the powers of the air, fire, water, and earth, you are now able to answer any questions correctly. The Nine of Hearts means yes; the Nine of Spades means no, and the Joker means maybe. To answer my questions, you must go through all dimensions of the universe, past, future, and return with accurate answers. So mote it be.*

XI. Go to each direction, starting by east, and say:

*I thank the guardians of the [insert direction] for your help today. I now close the portal of the [insert direction].*

XII. Go to the west of the altar, face east, and say:

*I thank the highest forces in the universe for allowing this work to happen. I now declare this temple closed.*

**Using the deck**

I. Sit down in a comfortable position and concentrate on what you want to know. Ask your question out loud, addressing the deck.

II. Shuffle the cards the best you can — the more shuffled, the better. While shuffling, ask the question again.

III. Put the deck in front of you like the following image.

**Figure 11. Playing card**

IV. Cut the deck two times from left to right.

**Figure 12. Cutting the deck**

V. Put the deck back together again, placing the piles on top of each other from left to right.

VI. Now start turning over the cards one by one in a left to right movement until you reach a yes, a no, or a maybe. For example, if you reach the yes first, this is your answer.

Don't ask the same question again. If you do this, you will probably get a different answer, and this will mess with your mind. You have to accept the first answer as the right one. This is how divination works. You can choose another method of shuffling and cutting the cards. It is up to you in case you have a better one.

# Free Writing

There is a method of divination called automatic writing that is similar to my free writing one but with a difference. To use the automatic writing, you take a pen or pencil, a sheet of paper, sit at a table, relax, and start writing what comes to your mind. This can work, and you should try it if you want. The method I am going to teach here is different because instead of you writing what comes to your mind, your hand automatic moves the pen, and you don't control when it starts and when it stops. I consider that this technique was developed by myself because this idea came to my mind without seeing anything similar anywhere before.

## Step by Step

I. If you wish, you can invoke some god that you believe in, or any other entity that you think can give you answers. Take a pen and sheet of paper. Sit down at a table or anywhere you can write comfortably.

II. Relax your body and mind. Forget about the rest of the world.

III. Put the sheet on the table and position the pen over it without putting much pressure.

IV. Give instructions on how you want to receive the answers. For example, say:

> *All the questions I ask here must be answered with a Y meaning yes and an N meaning no.*

V. Close your eyes and ask your question aloud.

Your hand will start moving in less than a minute. Don't put much pressure on the pen.

VI. After you finished, open your eyes and see if you got a Y or an N. This is your answer.

# CHAPTER 8

# EVOCATIONS

There is some confusion involving invocations and evocations, and one may use these two terms in the wrong way. Invocation is when you call an entity, but you don't ask for it to manifest to you in any way; evocation is when you explicitly demand the entity to manifest in an audible or visible form. Evocations have the advantage of being more intense since you can feel, hear, or see the spirit through the black mirror, candle flame, incense smoke, etc. Of course, the intensity of these effects is limited by your sensitive capacity, so you may evoke a spirit and don't feel, see, or hear anything. Some spells in this book are similar to evocations due to the ritual form, but since you were not instructed to wait for any kind of manifestation or ask for it, I classified them as invocations, although you may feel or hear something.

In this chapter, we are going to learn how to evoke Lucifer, Michael, and Lilith. The first two were chosen to be here because they are spirits that demand more attention, and although you can summon them using common methods, you probably will not get any results. Lilith is relatively easy to evoke, but she is hard to deal with, and some precautions must be taken.

# Lucifer

I would generally start this paragraph explaining what Lucifer is, his powers, etc., but I decided not to do so. Why? Because it is very hard to make contact with this spirit, and no one can really tell what Lucifer's real story is. I can only say things that are not directly dependent on him. For example, I can say that he is not the king of hell because we know hell doesn't exist; he is also not Satan at all because these two creatures have two different stories, and, to be frank, I am not sure if Satan exists either. It is also safe to say that Lucifer is an incredibly powerful spirit, well-known on the astral plane, and respected by the greatest entities. Many spirits, like kings and princes, are obedient to him.

Lucifer made his name and became the most famous angel between both humans and spirits. King, Prince, Imperator are among his titles, always being the greatest of them. The more important a spirit is, the more difficult it is to contact them. That explains why evoking Lucifer requires so much work and dedication. Or you devote yourself to him, or he will not notice your existence.

The instructions given below are to be strictly followed; otherwise, you are likely to fail.

## Worshiping Lucifer

Approaching Lucifer means to show him that you deserve his attention, and there is no better way to do this than worshiping him. It means that for a certain amount of days preceding the actual evocation, you have to forget all the other spirits you work with and focus your attention on Lucifer only. If you read this book from the beginning, you already know that you show devotion to a spirit through prayers and offerings, but with Lucifer, you should consider only the prayer part.

## No Offerings and No Banishing

Yes, you got it right. Lucifer is different, and no offerings are required when trying to make the first contact with him. Maybe later, when a bond is created between you two, he may ask something from you; for now, only prayers and a little self-sacrifice that I will explain later are necessary. Banishing rituals are also out of the question. While it is advisable to finish an evocation banishing the energies present at the place, with Lucifer, it is not necessary; actually, I don't believe high spirits like kings, princes, dukes should be banished since they tend to go away immediately after you gave them the license to depart. Lucifer should not even be invited to leave; he will do this by himself, don't worry.

## Pre-Ritual

For seven days before the ritual, you must recite a prayer to Lucifer. This should be made at the same hour every day. So, if on the first day you recited the prayer at 8 PM, the next six days, you will do it at 8 PM. You should also go without eating meat for seven days plus the hours till the ritual. This is a sacrifice you do in order to purify yourself. It is unlike Lucifer will talk to you if you are impure.

I. The prayer

*Hêlêl, Heylel, the Shining One, the Light Bearer.*

*Phosphorus, the Morning Star.*

*Heosphoros, the dawn bringer.*

*Great and Powerful Lucifer, the Light Bringer.*

*You who was wronged and profaned by humanity.*

*You who are respected and feared by spirits.*

*King, Prince, Imperator, and all the other names and titles you may want to be called.*

*O Mighty and Powerful Lucifer, your power and your glory are above all humans.*

*I call you, and I beg that you hear me.*

*Let me walk under your protection so no enemies will ever be able to reach me.*

*Send me your light and your knowledge; make me a wise man.*

*I invite you into my life, and I accept your glory.*

*Make me stronger and feared; make me healthy and lucky.*

*Make me see what I cannot see; make me able to feel your presence and hear your voice.*

*O Great and Powerful Lucifer, wronged and profaned by humanity.*

*Guide me and make me your protégé.*

*Hail Lucifer. Amen.*

II. After the prayer, meditate with Lucifer for ten minutes.

## The Ritual

After seven days of prayers and purification, you are ready to evoke Lucifer on the eighth day. The evocation must take place at 5 o'clock in the morning, so you start preparing the place some minutes before.

## Things you will need

- Incense. Choose one of these: morning star, sandalwood, lavender, cedarwood.
- Three white candles.
- The seal of Lucifer.

## Temple arrangements

I. Choose a quiet and clean place where you can be comfortable and relaxed.

II. Since you will be sitting on the floor and you have to be fully relaxed, you must have some cushions where you can sit on.

III. The altar must be prepared on the floor or a small table in front of you because you need to look at the seal while vibrating the name of Lucifer.

IV. Remove unnecessary things from the place.

V. Low light is always recommended. As in this ritual, three candles are used, there is no need to use electric light.

## Cleansing the space and setting up the altar

I. Burn an incense stick, and holding it, go to the east, facing east. Say:

*In the name of Lucifer, the Light Bearer, may this place be consecrated and purified.*

*I command all energies, evil or good, to leave this place right now.*

*This is the temple of Lucifer, where you are not allowed to stay.*

II. Spread incense smoke around the place.

III. Set up the altar with the triangle, candles, incense, and the seal of Lucifer. No circle must be made inside the triangle because it is not intended to hold him but to help him to manifest.

82  Evocations

IV. Put a candle on each edge of the triangle. Incense should be placed on its right and left sides.

V. Put the seal of Lucifer inside of it.

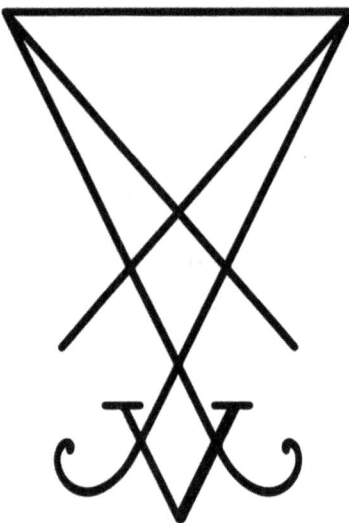

**Figure 13. The seal of Lucifer**

**Evoking**

I. Light the incense and candles.

II. Sit down in a comfortable position.

III. Recite the same prayer to Lucifer used at the beginning of this ritual.

IV. Gaze at the seal and vibrate the name of Lucifer for two minutes.

V. Now evoke Lucifer by saying the following conjuration seven times:

*O Great Lucifer, I have done all that is necessary to welcome you.*

*This is the temple that I have prepared for you.*

*I invite you to join me. Please reveal yourself to me.*

*Let me see, hear, or feel you.*

*Grant me the joy of your presence.*

*Come Lucifer. Come. Come. Come.*

VI. Close your eyes and meditate with Lucifer; visualize his seal in your mind.

Lucifer will guide you from this point. He will decide the best way to manifest himself to you. Maybe you will only be able to feel his presence but not listen to him.

VII. After he is gone, thank him with your own words. Note that I said after he is gone, that is, he decides when he should leave; you don't send him away.

# Michael

Michael is one of the four main archangels of God. He rules the fire element and is also the Archangel of the Sun (or Mercury) and the Archangel of Hod, a sphere of the Tree of Life. Michael is a warrior, and in the Christian tradition, he is described as the one who led God's armies against Satan. He is seen as the opposite of Lucifer, the one who remained faithfully on God's side.

You must already know that summoning an archangel is not an easy task. They lead the universe among the other angels, demons, and spirits; they are in charge of planets and spheres, so they will not come to those that are not fully prepared or are impure. This means that the same devotion given to Lucifer has to be given to Michael as well.

Some people say angels are arrogant creatures when they are evoked. Although I don't think this is a rule, you may find an angel that is not willing to talk to you or is not used to talking to humans, but this is not the case of Michael. He knows humans very well, and he is used to hearing prayers every single day.

## Pre-Ritual

I am afraid that just like in the Lucifer ritual, you also have to go without eating meat for seven days to summon Michael. To succeed in contacting powerful spirits like these two, your body must be pure. As said in Chapter 1, you should do this before every evocation. Of course, seven days without meat is only required with spirits that are harder to contact; with the other ones, 24 hours is enough.

The following prayer must be recited for seven consecutive days preceding the ritual:

*O Mighty and Powerful Michael, Archangel of Shemesh, Archangel of Hod, Ruler of the Fire Element, Great Prince, Warrior of God, Saint Michael, Protector of Israel.*

*You who carry a flaming sword and no enemy dare to fight with you.*

*Guide me and protect me against all my enemies; make them feel your power.*

*I know I am only a human, I know that compared to you I am nobody, I know I am weak.*

*But I ask you to teach me how I can be stronger, how I can make my enemies fear me, how I can be a warrior like you.*

*So that, I will be able to be by your side, I will be able to walk with you, Holy Michael.*

*I do not wish to be your servant, but I do wish to be your friend.*

*Hail Archangel Michael. Amen.*

## The Ritual

Unlike Lucifer, Michael doesn't have a particular hour to be called, but I highly recommend that you also summon him at 5'oclock in the morning. Otherwise, you should choose a time when everything is calm, with no street traffic, noise in the neighborhood, etc.

**Things you will need**

- Look for any Saint Michael or Archangel Michael incense; otherwise, use frankincense.
- Four yellow candles.
- The seal of Michael.

**Temple arrangements**

I. Choose a quiet and clean place where you can be comfortable and relaxed.

II. Since you will be sitting on the floor and you have to be fully relaxed, you must have some cushions where you can sit on.

III. The altar must be prepared on the floor or a small table in front of you because you need to look at the seal while vibrating the name of Michael.

IV. Remove unnecessary things from the place.

V. Low light is always recommended. As in this ritual, three candles are used, there is no need to use electric light.

**Cleansing the space and setting up the altar**

I. Light a candle, and holding it, go to the south. Draw in the air the Invoking Pentagram of Fire.

**Figure 14. The Invoking Pentagram of Fire**

II. Say:

*In the name of the Great Archangel Michael, and through the fire element, I purify this place.*

*All energies, evil or good, must leave right now.*

III. Michael is the ruler of the south, so the altar must be placed in the south. Set it up in front of where you will sit, with the triangle, candles, incense, and the seal of Michael. No circle must be made inside the triangle because it is not intended to hold him but to help him to manifest.

IV. Put a candle on each edge of the triangle. Incense should be placed on its right and left sides.

V. Put the seal of Michael inside of it.

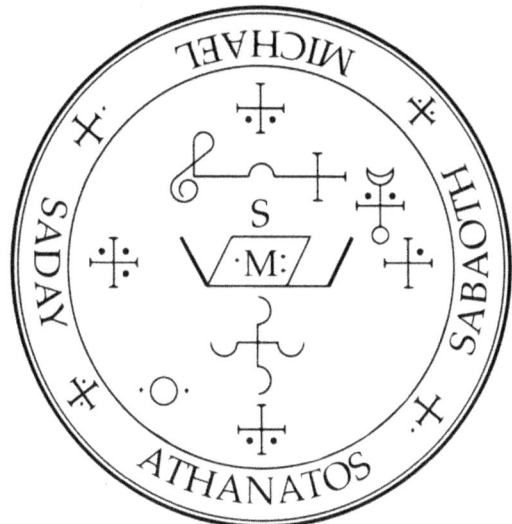

Figure 15. The seal of Michael

**Evoking**

I. Light the candles and incense.

II. Sit down in a comfortable position.

III. Recite the same prayer to Michael used at the beginning of this ritual.

IV. Gaze at the seal and vibrate the name of Michael for two minutes.

V. Start the evocation by saying the following conjuration seven times:

*O Great and Powerful Michael, I invoke you.*

*Archangel of Fire ruling in the south, I invoke you.*

*Archangel of Shemesh, I invoke you.*

*Archangel of Hod, I invoke you.*

*Michael, warrior of God, most powerful angel.*

*I invite you to join me in this temple specially prepared for you.*

*Come and reveal yourself to me because I prepared my body and soul to be in tune with your purity and your glory.*

VI. Stay in silence, waiting for Michael. Every detail is important at this moment. The temperature of the place may rise or fall; the incense smoke may change its direction; you may feel someone's presence. If you are sensitive enough, you should be able to hear his voice, but seeing is another story. If you want to see a spirit during an evocation, you must use a black mirror, because to manifest on the physical plane is too hard for them.

VII. After he is gone, thank him with your own words.

# Lilith

For a detailed description of Lilith, see Chapter 3.

A kind of preliminary rite where you express the desire to communicate directly with her should precede an evocation of Lilith. She is not like most other spirits, and she probably will not welcome you with "what do you want from me?"; she is more likely to be a little bit rude and questions you about a good reason why you are summoning her and what you have to offer. You must read a prayer for three consecutive days before the ritual in order to introduce yourself to her. You are more likely to have success if she previously knows with whom she is working with.

## Approaching Lilith

I. First, you need to draw the seal of Lilith (Figure 3) on a blank paper.

II. Looking at the seal, recite the following prayer for three days before the ritual:

*Lilith, Laylah, powerful spirit of many names and many titles, I come before you willing to receive your advice and teachings in the areas of witchcraft, sex, seduction, and everything else you master.*

*May there always be peace and harmony between us.*

*Hail Laylah. Amen.*

## The Ritual

Lilith should be evoked after midnight for better results. Although not required, a ritual taking place on a full moon day and under the moonlight would be a perfect combination for a powerful manifestation.

**Things you will need**

- Incense: jasmine, rose, herbs, or any of the Lilith incense that can be found in esoteric shops.
- Three red candles.
- Red rose petals to decorate the altar (optional).
- The seal of Lilith.

**Setting up the altar**

I. Set up the altar with the Triangle of the Art, candles, incense, and red rose petals.

II. Put a candle on each edge of the triangle. Incense should be placed on its right and left sides.

III. Put the rose petals around the candles.

IV. Put the seal of Lilith inside the triangle.

**Evoking**

I. Perform a banishing in the name of Lilith:

*In the name of Layil, mistress of the night, of wrath, and storms, I command all negativity to leave this place. By the power of Layil, mistress of destruction and punishment, may this place be blessed and I purified.*

*PROCUL, O PROCUL ESTE PROFANI. Profane and unclean spirits go away.*

II. Cast a circle.

III. Put hands together and say:

*In the name of Lilith, I declare this temple open.*

IV. Start the evocation by saying:

*Lilith, Laylah, Darkat, Layil, I invoke you.*

*Mother of Seduction, Mistress of the Night, and all the other names you may want to be called, I invoke you.*

*Come holy angel of prostitution and join me in this sacred temple.*

*Come peacefully, visibly, affably, and answer all my requests.*

*Open the doors of your world to me and make me understand all the mysteries of sex, passion, seduction, witchcraft, and all the other areas you master.*

*Laylah, hear me and come from any part of the world you may be.*

*I call you. I call you. I call you.*

Repeat this conjuration two more times. Lilith will not take long to manifest. If you can hear her voice, stay calm and don't argue with her. Remember, she is the one who can teach you many things and not the contrary.

V. After she answered all your questions, thank her with your own words and gently ask her to always come quickly when she is summoned.

VI. Close the circle.

VII. Perform the Banishing Ritual of the Pentagram.

Note: Lilith should not be your first choice for help. Even if you have a peaceful experience with her, remember that she has a wild nature. A few years ago, it came to my knowledge, a story of a teenager who recklessly consecrated his unborn baby brother to Lilith. A few days later, the boy's mother began having complications and eventually had an abortion. Although I can't confirm the veracity of this case, it is something that could happen.

# CHAPTER 9

# PLANETARY MAGIC

When I was starting the study of magic, I didn't even know how important planets are to our lives. I have always been passionate about astronomy, but I always ignored astrology. Signs, planets position, hours, days, colors, had never meant anything to me until I discovered that planets are, in fact, the home of all spirits that we know. They are part of a complex system where the astral plane is organized and by which our world is directly influenced. Examples of well-known spirits and their planets are Gabriel (Moon), Michael (Sun), Sachiel (Jupiter), Anael (Venus).

Planetary Magic is a field with a lot of information that could not be completely detailed in this book, which is intended to be practical and easy to follow. In this chapter, we are going to take a brief look at this subject, addressing the main points so that you can begin to practice this type of magic.

# The Seven Planets and Their Characteristics

In astronomy, we have the following planets in our solar system: Mercury, Venus, Earth, Mars, Jupiter, Saturn, Uranus, and Neptune. The Sun is our star and the Moon the Earth' satellite. This is the configuration of the solar system on the physical plane; however, this is a little bit different when we talk about planetary magic. In astrology, seven planets dictate our lives; they are Saturn, Jupiter, Mars, Sun, Venus, Mercury, and Moon. As you can see, the Sun is considered a planet and also is the Moon, which is the most complex of them, as you will see later. Earth is not taken into consideration because we live here, and so we can observe all the planets except our own.

Each planet has a different energy representing many aspects of our lives. For example, we have the Sun with its healing powers; Mercury ruling over the intellect; Venus responsible for sexual matters. Below you have a complete list with all the powers of the seven planets.

**Saturn:** principles, maturity, obligation, stability, organization, ancestors, responsibility, law, restriction, prudence, structure, age, hard work, patience, discipline, pragmatism, command, caution, punctuality, administration, obstacles, deprivation, hierarchy, foundation, repair, reality, duty, honor, training.

**Jupiter:** travels, journeys, amplitude, wisdom, abundance, liberty, philanthropy, advice, fairness, fortune, blessing, new beginnings, ethic, opportunity, happiness, consultation, philosophy, altruism, beliefs, optimism, wealth.

**Mars:** sports, will, energy, action, ardor, rush, courage, insistence, sexual desire, exercise, encounter, combat, trial, adventure.

**Sun:** advancement, authority, determination, decisions, recognition, fame, success, projects, dignity, self-confidence, plans, strength, vitality, thoughts, achievement, creativity.

**Venus:** communities, balance, romanticism, flirt, diplomacy, meditation, love, styles, visits, social activities, affection, beauty, delights, companionship, art, comfort.

**Mercury:** pursuits, learning, dialogues, discussions, instruction, speeches, talks, teaching, correspondences, information, ideas, transportation, literature, intellectual, contracts, language, criticism, studying, editing, conferences, writing, traffic, lectures, communication.

**Moon:** tides, relaxation, feelings, emotions, receptivity, meditation, nostalgia, tranquility, family, fertility, isolation, subconscious, calmness, nurturing, memories, security, babies.

Each planet has a day of the week it rules and non-consecutive hours during a day it also rules. The hour is always more important than the day, and their combination is a perfect choice. For example, if someone wishes to work with the Sun, the best day is Sunday during one of the Sun hours. But if you are not available during its hours, you should choose any other day but always respecting the Sun hours. The planetary hours are not the same every day, and they are calculated based on your location. You can find many sites that will give you the hours for a specific day based on where you are located; there are also some Android apps that will provide you with this information even more precisely.

Other characteristics of the planets are colors and symbols. The colors you are going to learn in this book are known as the Queen Scale, which represents the level of the archangels. All operations made at this level will reflect here on Earth, so you don't need to learn the other levels for now. The planet symbols are also an important part of planetary magic; they carry a mystical power and are used in many magical operations, such as evocations of planetary spirits. Below you have a table containing the day of the planets, colors, and symbols.

Table 3. The characteristics of the planets

| Planet | Day | Color | Symbol |
|---|---|---|---|
| Saturn | Saturday | Black | ♄ |
| Jupiter | Thursday | Blue | ♃ |
| Mars | Tuesday | Scarlet Red | ♂ |
| Sun | Sunday | Yellow | ☉ |
| Venus | Friday | Emerald | ♀ |
| Mercury | Wednesday | Orange | ☿ |
| Moon | Monday | Violet | ☾ |

If you arrived here after reading the last chapter, you must have noticed that in the invocation of Michael, we referred to the Sun as Shemesh. This is the Hebrew name of the Sun, and all the other planets have theirs as well. In the following table, you can see the Hebrew name of the seven planets.

Table 4. Names of the planets in Hebrew

| Planet | Hebrew Name |
|---|---|
| Saturn | Shabbathai |
| Jupiter | Tzedek |
| Mars | Madim |
| Sun | Shemesh |
| Venus | Nogah |
| Mercury | Kobab |
| Moon | Levanah |

Each planet is part of a bigger structure called Sephiroth or Sephira (singular). The Sephiroth are referred to as spheres that are emanations of the divine power. This is a simplistic explanation of these complex structures intended only to serve as an introduction to the next subject about the different forces ruling the spheres and planets. Below you have a table relating the planets to their corresponding spheres.

Table 5. Planets and spheres

| Planet | Sphere |
|---|---|
| Saturn | Binah |
| Jupiter | Chesed |
| Mars | Geburah |
| Sun | Tiphareth |
| Venus | Netzach |
| Mercury | Hod |
| Moon | Yesod |
| Earth | Malkuth |

# Power Hierarchy

There are four levels of power to be considered when working with planets; they are Divine, Archangelic, Angelic, and Earth. The Divine levels are the spheres of light where a specific name of God (divine name) manifests, and below God, there is the archangel of the sphere. The Archangelic level is represented by the planetary archangels; the Angelic by the intelligences and the Earth level corresponds to the spirits of the planets.

The archangels of the spheres are above the ones of the planets. They have more power and can do anything at any level since they are rulers of the Sephiroth. It doesn't mean that you should go directly ask something to these spirits. The planetary archangels are specialized according to the characteristics of their planets, and so they can give you what you want faster.

Intelligence is an angel that controls the spirit of the planet. They tell them what to do because the spirits alone are blind forces. When you want a more reflective approach to the planet's powers, you usually call the intelligence. When you want material things, like getting a job, a new car, or even attract someone you love, you should work with the spirit. Bear in mind the intelligences can be difficult forces to deal with, and the spirits are even more challenging. When evoking the spirit, you must always call the intelligence first, and when evoking the intelligence, it is advisable to call the archangel of the planet.

## Table 6. Powers ruling the planets 1

| Sphere | Name of God | Archangel | Planet |
|---|---|---|---|
| Binah | YHVH Elohim<br>אלהים יהוה | Tzaphkiel<br>צפקיאל | Saturn |
| Chesed | El<br>אל | Tzadkiel<br>צדקיאל | Jupiter |
| Geburah | Elohim Gibor<br>גביר אלהים | Kamael<br>כמאל | Mars |
| Tiphareth | YHVH Eloah ve-Daath<br>ודעת אלוה יהוה | Raphael<br>רפאל | Sun |
| Netzach | YHVH Tzabaoth<br>צבאות יהוה | Haniel<br>האניאל | Venus |
| Hod | Elohim Tzabaoth<br>בצאות אלהים | Michael<br>מיכאל | Mercury |
| Yesod | Shaddai El Chai<br>חי אל שדי | Gabriel<br>גבריאל | Moon |
| Malkuth | Adonai Ha Aretz<br>מלך אדני | Sandalphon<br>סנדלפון | Earth |

### Table 7. Powers ruling the planets 2

| Planet | Archangel | Intelligence | Spirit |
|---|---|---|---|
| Saturn | Cassiel<br>כסיאל | Agiel<br>אגיאל | Zazel<br>זזאל |
| Jupiter | Sachiel<br>סחיאל | Yophiel<br>יופיאל | Hismael<br>הסמאל |
| Mars | Zamael<br>זמאל | Graphiel<br>גראפיאל | Bartzabel<br>ברצבאל |
| Sun | Michael<br>מיכאל | Nakhiel<br>נכיאל | Sorath<br>סורת |
| Venus | Anael<br>אנאל | Hagiel<br>הגיאל | Qedemel<br>קדמאל |
| Mercury | Raphael<br>רפאל | Tiriel<br>תיריאל | Taphthartharath<br>תפתרתרת |
| Moon | Gabriel<br>גבריאל | Malkah Be Tarshishim va A'ad Be Ruah Shehaqim<br>מלכא ועד בתרשישים שהקים ברוה | Chasmodai<br>חשמודאי |

Note that Raphael is the archangel of both Tiphareth (sphere) and Mercury (planet); Michael is the archangel of Hod and the Sun; Gabriel is the archangel of Yesod and the Moon. Taking Raphael as an example, the difference between the one ruling a planet and the one ruling a sphere is their powers.

Raphael ruling Mercury has his powers according to the characteristics of the planet, while Raphael ruling Tiphareth has unlimited power.

The Moon is the most complex planet because it has many mansions, and each one of them has its own intelligence and spirit. Malkah Be Tarshishim va A'ad Be Ruah Shehaqim is the intelligence of the intelligences of the Moon. The spirit of the spirits of the Moon is Schad Barschemoth ha Shartathan, but some ancient books refer to Chasmodai or Hasmodai as the spirit of the Moon. For the sake of simplicity, I preferred to use Chasmodai as the spirit of the Moon because when we learn how to make planetary seals, it will be a lot difficult to write the name of both intelligence of the intelligences and spirit of the spirits in a small piece of paper.

# Evoking Planetary Spirits

The first thing to do before summoning a planetary spirit is to decide what you want from them. You are not going to call a spirit to chat with you or to ask questions that you can answer by reading a book. You should only ask their help with things that you can't get by yourself or demand hard work. The second thing is to define if your problem is more material or spiritual. The rule is material = spirit and spiritual = intelligence or archangel.

You don't call the archangels of the spheres in a ritual of evocation. These creatures take care of the whole universe and not only of our solar system. You will get better results working with the intelligences and spirits of the planets.

Every magic operation involving planets must take place in the hour of the specific planet. Don't ignore it, or the energy you will get for your work will be considerably small.

## Seals of the Planets, Intelligences, and Spirits

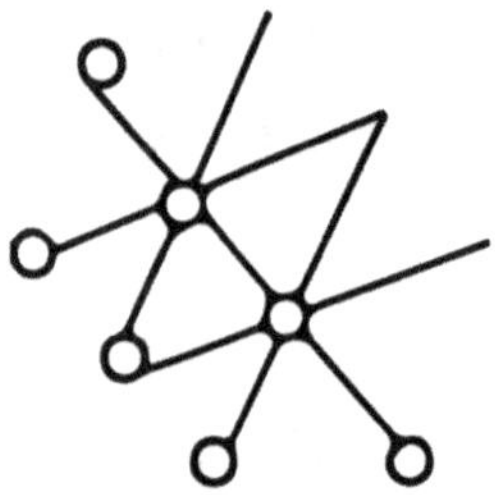

Figure 16. The seal of Saturn

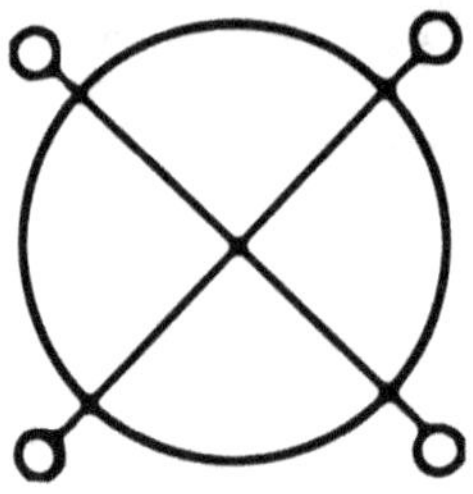

Figure 17. The seal of Jupiter

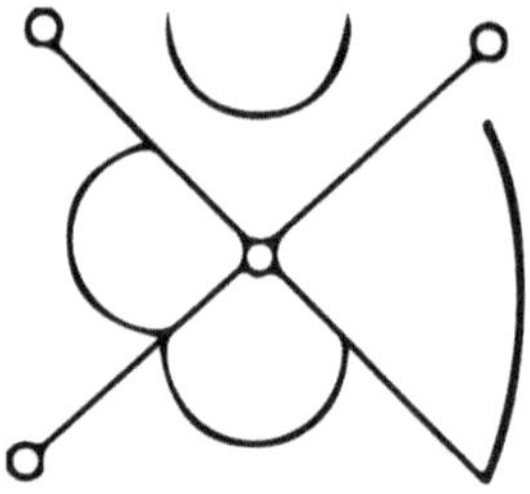

Figure 18. The seal of Mars

Figure 19. The seal of the Sun

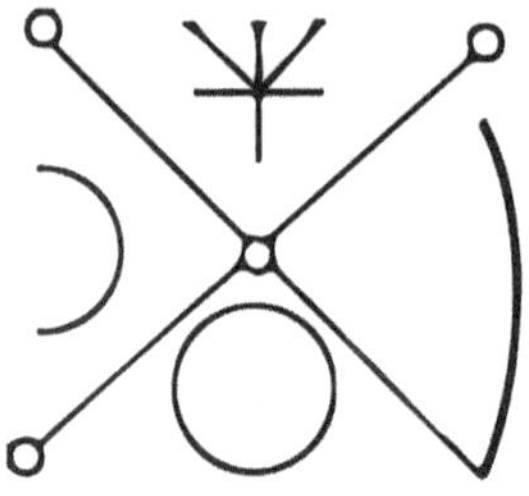

Figure 20. The seal of Venus

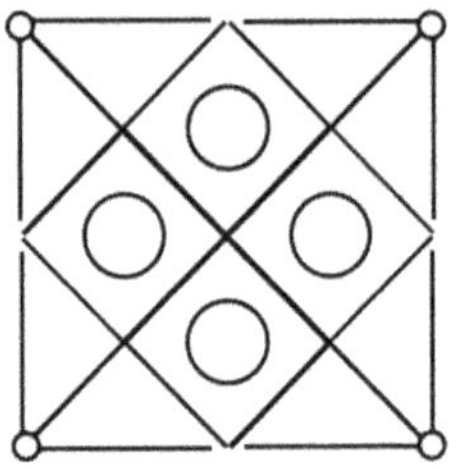

Figure 21. The seal of Mercury

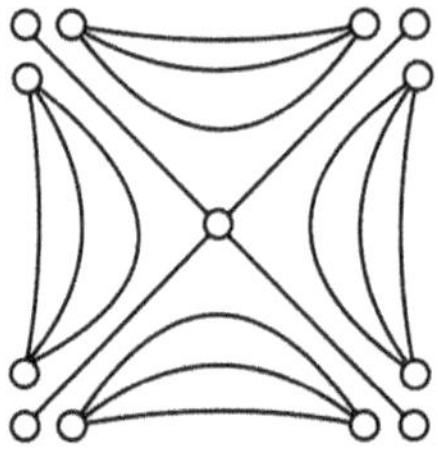

Figure 22. The seal of the Moon

Below you have the seals of the intelligences and spirits, respectively.

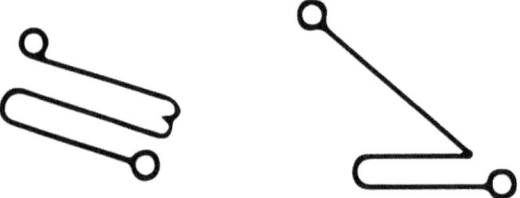

Figure 23. The seals of Agiel and Zazel

Planetary Magic 103

Figure 24. The seals of Yophiel and Hismael

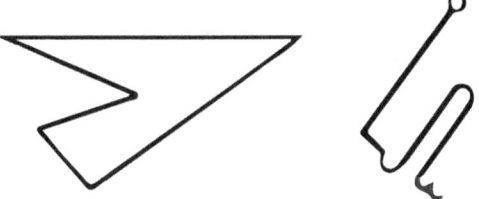

Figure 25. The seals of Graphiel and Bartzabel

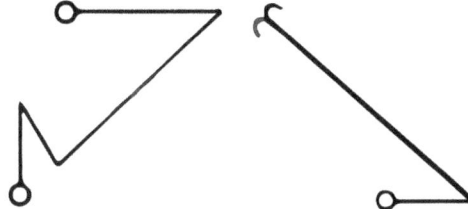

Figure 26. The seals of Nakhiel and Sorath

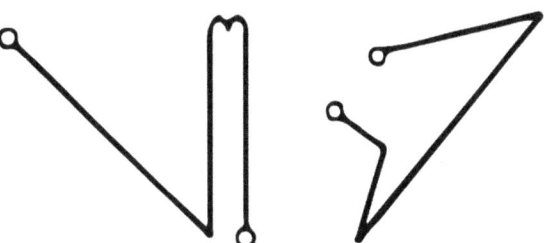

Figure 27. The seals of Hagiel and Qedemel

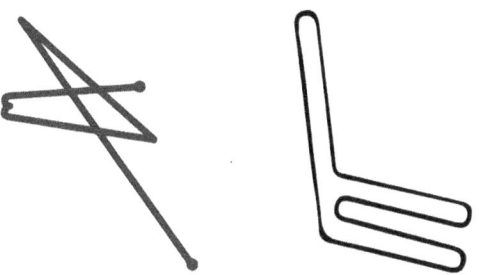

Figure 28. The seals of Tiriel and Taphthartharath

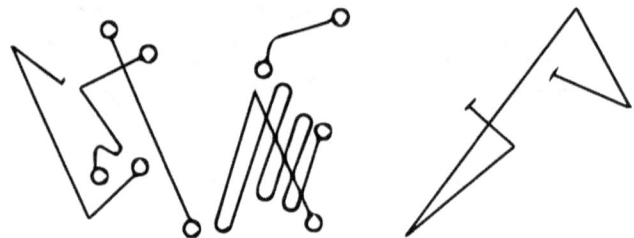

Figure 29. The seals of the Intelligence of the Moon and Chasmodai

## Things You Will Need

- Three candles in the proper color of the planet.
- Incense according to the following table:

Table 8. Planetary incense

| Planet | Incense |
|---|---|
| Saturn | Musk, myrrh, civet, patchouli, sage. |
| Jupiter | Cedar, nutmeg, honeysuckle, mace, lemon, saffron. |
| Mars | Dragon's blood, pine, cypress, benzoin, tobacco, coriander, cumin, ginger, pepper. |
| Sun | Frankincense, orange, acacia, calendula, cinnamon, bay, saffron. |
| Venus | Rose, myrtle, jasmine, benzoin, apple, chamomile, cardamom, gardenia, hyacinth, lilac, magnolia, vanilla, licorice, musk. |
| Mercury | Mace, almond, storax, sandalwood, lavender, benzoin, bergamot, mint, sage, sweet pea, lily of the valley. |
| Moon | Jasmine, poppy, myrtle, camphor, sandalwood, night-blooming cereus, opium. |

## Step by Step

I. Draw the seal of the planet on A4 paper using the proper color. On a small paper, you separately draw the seal of the spirit and intelligence, also using the color of the planet.

II. Set up the altar with the Triangle of the Art, candles, and incense. The triangle must be placed over the seal of the planet.

III. Put a candle on each edge of the triangle. Incense should be placed on its right and left sides.

IV. Put the seal of the spirit and intelligence inside the triangle.

V. Perform the Banishing Ritual of the Pentagram.

Note: some sources say that you should perform the Greater Ritual of the Hexagram as well to invoke planetary energy. I don't think it is necessary because the ritual I describe here is to be performed in the hour of the planet. The GRH was created by the Golden Dawn in 1888, and planetary magic is much older than that.

VI. Light the candles and incense.

VII. Cast a circle.

VIII. Evoke the archangel of the planet:

> *O Great and Powerful [insert the name of the archangel], archangel of [insert the name of the planet], in the name of [insert the name of God of the sphere], I invoke you. Come and reveal yourself to me.*

IX. Evoke the intelligence of the planet:

> *O Great and Powerful [insert the name of the intelligence], Intelligence of [insert the name of the planet], in the name of [insert the name of the archangel], I invoke you. Come and reveal yourself to me.*

X. Evoke the spirit of the planet:

*O Great and Powerful [insert the name of the spirit], spirit of [insert the name of the planet], in the name of [insert the name of the intelligence], I invoke you. Come ready to answer my questions and fulfill my commands because I invoke you in the name of [insert the name of the intelligence].*

XI. When you feel the presence of the spirit, give him your commands. Never forget to ask him to complete his task without causing harm to you, your family, your friends, or anyone else.

XII. Thanking the spirits

*I thank you, O Great Archangel of [insert the name of the planet], for your presence in this rite. You can go in peace.*

Repeat the same for the intelligence and spirit.

XIII. Perform the Qabalistic Cross.

# The Seven Olympic Spirits

The only source about the Olympic Spirits is the Arbatel of Magic, dated 1575, translated by Robert Turner in 1655. No other book had previously mentioned these spirits. I also don't know any book after that date that adds something different about them. Since our focus is to learn how to evoke the Olympic Spirits and the fact the Arbatel remains our primary source of knowledge about them, I will quote here exactly what is said about these seven spirits in the translation of that book by Robert Turner in 1655. It will give us, in fact, all the necessary information that we need to summon each one of them. I had to make changes to the original translation because the text has an old writing style, and also some words are written in their archaic form.

"They are called Olympic Spirits which do inhabit in the firmament and in the stars of the firmament. The office of these spirits is to declare destinies and to administer fatal charms, so far forth as God pleases to permit them.

There are seven different governments of the Spirits of Olympus by whom God has appointed the whole frame and universe of this world to be governed, and their visible stars are Aratron, Bethor, Phaleg, Och, Hagith, Ophiel, and Phul. Every one of these has under him a mighty militia in the firmament.

So there are 186 Olympic Provinces in the whole universe, wherein the seven governors do exercise their powers, all of which are elegantly set forth in astronomy. But here, it will be explained in what manner these princes and powers may be drawn into communication.

Aratron appears in the first hour of Saturday, and very truly gives answers concerning his provinces and provincials. So likewise, the rest of them appear in their respective days and hours. Also, every one of them rules for 490 years. The beginning of their government, in the year 60 before the nativity of Christ, was the beginning of the administration of Bethor, and it lasted until the year 430 after our Lord Christ. To whom succeeded Phaleg, until the year 920. Then began Och and continued until the year 1410, and thenceforth Hagith rules until the year 1900.

The governor Aratron has in his power those things which he does naturally, that is, the things which in astronomy are ascribed to the power of Saturn. What he does of his own free will is:

1. He can convert anything into a stone in a moment, either animal or plant, retaining the same object to the sight.

2. He converts treasures into coles, and coles into treasure.

3. He gives familiar spirits with a definite power.

4. He teaches alchemy, magic, and physic.

5. He reconciles the subterranean spirits to men and makes men hairy.

6. He causes one to be invisible.

7. The barren he makes fruitful and gives a long life.

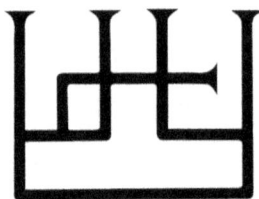

**Figure 30. The seal of Aratron**

He has under him 49 kings, 42 princes, 35 presidents, 28 dukes, 21 ministers standing before him, 14 familiars, seven messengers. He commands 36000 legions of spirits.

Bethor governs those things which are ascribed to Jupiter. He soon comes after being called. Those who are dignified with his character, he raises to very great honors and may give large treasures. He reconciles the spirits of the air, so they will give true answers, transport precious stones from place to place, and make medicines to work miraculously in their effects. He also gives familiars of the firmament and prolongs life to 700 years if God will.

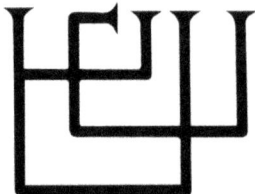

**Figure 31. The seal of Bethor**

He has under him 42 kings, 35 princes, 28 dukes, 21 counsellors, 14 ministers, seven messengers, 29000 legions of spirits.

Phaleg rules those things which are attributed to Mars, the Prince of Peace. Those who possess his character, he raises to great honors in warlike affairs.

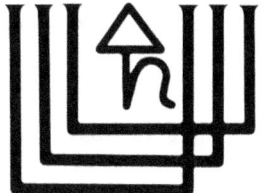

**Figure 32. The seal of Phaleg**

*Och governs solar things. He gives 600 years with perfect health. He bestows great wisdom, gives the most excellent spirits, teaches perfect medicines. He converts all things into most pure gold and precious stones, gives gold, and a purse springing with gold. Those who are dignified with his character, he makes them be worshiped as a deity by the kings of the whole world.*

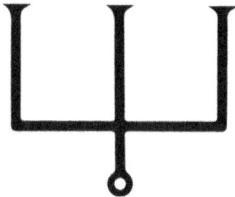

**Figure 33. The seal of Och**

*He has under him 36536 legions. He administrates all things alone, and all his spirits serve him by centuries.*

*Hagith governs those things attributed to Venus. Those who are dignified with his character, he makes very fair and to be adorned with all beauty. He converts copper into gold in a moment and gold into copper. He gives spirits that do faithfully serve those to whom they have been assigned.*

**Figure 34. The seal of Hagith**

*He has 4000 legions of spirits, and over every thousand, he ordains kings for their appointed seasons.*

*Ophiel is the governor of those things attributed to Mercury. His character is this.*

**Figure 35. The seal of Ophiel**

*His spirits are 100000 legions. He easily gives familiar spirits, teaches all arts, and those who are dignified with his character, he makes them be able in a moment to convert quicksilver into the philosopher stone.*

*Phul changes all metals into silver, in word, and deed. He governs lunar things. He heals dropsy, gives spirits of the water who do serve men in a corporeal and visible form, and makes men live 300 years."*

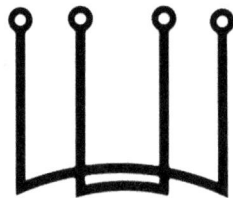

**Figure 36. The seal of Phul**

*Arbatel of Magic (translated by Robert Turner, 1655)*

The above explanation about the seven Olympic Spirits (Aratron, Bethor, Phaleg, Och, Hagith, Ophiel, Phul) extracted from the Arbatel of Magic is enough to understand how incredibly powerful these spirits are. We can see this by the number of other powerful spirits like kings who are under their command. In Goetia, we have kings ruling 50, 70 legions of spirits. Ophiel alone rules 100000 legions. You must respect every spirit you work with, but when working with these, add a few more doses of it.

# Evoking the Olympic Spirits

As you already know, every planetary magical operation must follow some rules like the hour of the planet, colors, and incense. For colors, check Table 3. For incense, check Table 8.

Table 9. The Olympic Spirits and their planets

| Spirit | Planet |
|---|---|
| Aratron | Saturn |
| Bethor | Jupiter |
| Phaleg | Mars |
| Och | Sun |
| Hagith | Venus |
| Ophiel | Mercury |
| Phul | Moon |

For this ritual, we are going to use something called Planetary Discs. These discs are made using the color of the planet and the corresponding flashing color. This system was developed by the Hermetic Order of the Golden Dawn.

Table 10. Flashing colors

| Color | Flashing Color |
|---|---|
| Black | White |
| Blue | Orange |
| Red | Green |
| Yellow | Violet |
| Green | Red |
| Orange | Blue |
| Violet | Yellow |

A planetary disc is a circle made of paper with 10 centimeters or 4 inches in diameter approximately. The background color is the color of the planet. In the center, the symbol of the planet must be drawn using the flashing color.

**Things you will need**

- Three candles in the color of the planet.
- Incense according to the planet.
- Planetary Disc.
- The seal of the Olympic Spirit.
- Accessories, such as cloths, rugs, curtains in the color of the planet.

**Pre-ritual**

I. Self-purification

Go without eating meat for 24 hours to purify your soul and take a bath before the ritual to cleanse your body.

II. Temple arrangements

Use curtains, rugs, cloths in the color of the planet at least at the altar. Colored light is the best option here. You can make one using white light and cellophane. You place cellophane in the proper color in front of white light, and the result will be light in the desired color.

III. Setting up the altar

Cover the altar with a cloth in the color of the planet. Place the triangle with a candle on each one of its edges. The incense should be placed on the right and left sides of the triangle.

Put the planetary disc inside the triangle and over it the seal of the Olympic Spirit. Note: in the Arbatel, the word character is used to refer to seals.

## The ritual

I. Perform the Banishing Ritual of the Pentagram.

Note: some sources say that you should perform the Greater Ritual of the Hexagram as well to invoke planetary energy. I don't think it is necessary because the ritual I describe here is to be performed in the hour of the planet. The GRH was created by the Golden Dawn in 1888, and planetary magic is much older than that.

II. Light the candles and incense.

III. Cast a circle.

IV. Put hands together and say:

*In the name of [insert the name of God of the sphere], I declare this temple open and ready to receive the energy of [insert the name of the planet].*

V. Begin the evocation:

*O Great [insert the name of the spirit], Olympic Spirit of [insert the name of the planet], ruling under the name of [insert the name of God of the sphere], and in the name of this same God, I invoke you. Appear before me right now and answer all my questions. Come without delay, peacefully and visibly. I speak in the name of the One who created all the things and to whom you are obedient. Come [insert the name of the spirit]. I invoke you.*

Repeat this conjuration seven times and wait for the spirit. If he doesn't appear, repeat it seven more times. Remember, you have less than an hour to finish the ritual.

The spirit may not come but send one of the millions of spirits under his command instead. It is just fine. The spirit will deliver all your requests to his master. To be sure about which spirit is present, you should ask for confirmation through the incense smoke or candle flame as soon as you notice someone's presence.

VI. After you are done, thank the spirit:

*O Great Olympic Spirit [insert the name of the spirit], I thank you for your presence. I hope you can fulfill all I have asked from you. You can go in peace to where you came from.*

OR

*I thank you, spirit under the command of [insert the name of the Olympic Spirit] for your presence. Go now and deliver my message to your master.*

VII. Close the temple:

*I now declare this temple of [insert the name of the planet] closed.*

VIII. Perform the Qabalistic Cross.

# Creating Planetary Seals

Planetary seals are seals created with the help of Magic Squares to represent something you wish to happen in your life. In other words, you are using the energy of a planet and the spirits ruling it to materialize your desire without you having to perform an evocation.

Planetary Magic Squares or Kameas are numbers arranged in a certain format representing the forces ruling a planet, including the planet itself. The sum of each row will result in a number called magic constant. Let's take a look at the square of Saturn.

Table 11. The square of Saturn

| 4 | 9 | 2 |
|---|---|---|
| 3 | 5 | 7 |
| 8 | 1 | 6 |

You can sum the numbers in any direction, and the result will be 15. Examples: 4+9+2=15; 2+5+8=15.

## Choosing the Right Planet

The first and most important thing to do is to select the right energy to work with. If you want money, you are not going to work with Venus because this planet has nothing to do with money. Choosing the wrong energy can cause you adverse effects. You can check the characteristics of each planet at the beginning of this chapter.

## Drawing the Magic Squares

Once again, I highly recommend that you do all the process in the hour of the planet. The squares must be drawn on a blank sheet of white paper after you exorcise it.

> *Creature of paper, I exorcise you and cleanse you. You are now purified and ready to be used in my magical work.*

**Table 12. The square of Jupiter**

| 4  | 14 | 15 | 1  |
|----|----|----|----|
| 9  | 7  | 6  | 12 |
| 5  | 11 | 10 | 8  |
| 16 | 2  | 3  | 13 |

**Table 13. The square of Mars**

| 11 | 24 | 7  | 20 | 3  |
|----|----|----|----|----|
| 4  | 12 | 25 | 8  | 16 |
| 17 | 5  | 13 | 21 | 9  |
| 10 | 18 | 1  | 14 | 22 |
| 23 | 6  | 19 | 2  | 15 |

**Table 14. The square of the Sun**

| 6  | 32 | 3  | 34 | 35 | 1  |
|----|----|----|----|----|----|
| 7  | 11 | 27 | 28 | 8  | 30 |
| 19 | 14 | 16 | 15 | 23 | 24 |
| 18 | 20 | 22 | 21 | 17 | 13 |
| 25 | 29 | 10 | 9  | 26 | 12 |
| 36 | 5  | 33 | 4  | 2  | 31 |

**Table 15. The square of Venus**

| 22 | 47 | 16 | 41 | 10 | 35 | 4  |
|----|----|----|----|----|----|----|
| 5  | 23 | 48 | 17 | 42 | 11 | 29 |
| 30 | 6  | 24 | 49 | 18 | 36 | 12 |
| 13 | 31 | 7  | 25 | 43 | 19 | 37 |
| 38 | 14 | 32 | 1  | 26 | 44 | 20 |
| 21 | 39 | 8  | 33 | 2  | 27 | 45 |
| 46 | 15 | 40 | 9  | 34 | 3  | 28 |

**Table 16. The square of Mercury**

| 8  | 58 | 59 | 5  | 4  | 62 | 63 | 1  |
|----|----|----|----|----|----|----|----|
| 49 | 15 | 14 | 52 | 53 | 11 | 10 | 56 |
| 41 | 23 | 22 | 44 | 45 | 19 | 18 | 48 |
| 32 | 34 | 35 | 29 | 28 | 38 | 39 | 25 |
| 40 | 26 | 27 | 37 | 36 | 30 | 31 | 33 |
| 17 | 47 | 46 | 20 | 21 | 43 | 42 | 24 |
| 9  | 55 | 54 | 12 | 13 | 51 | 50 | 16 |
| 64 | 2  | 3  | 61 | 60 | 6  | 7  | 57 |

**Table 17. The square of the Moon**

| 37 | 78 | 29 | 70 | 21 | 62 | 13 | 54 | 5  |
|----|----|----|----|----|----|----|----|----|
| 6  | 38 | 79 | 30 | 71 | 22 | 63 | 14 | 46 |
| 47 | 7  | 39 | 80 | 31 | 72 | 23 | 55 | 15 |
| 16 | 48 | 8  | 40 | 81 | 32 | 64 | 24 | 56 |
| 57 | 17 | 49 | 9  | 41 | 73 | 33 | 65 | 25 |
| 26 | 58 | 18 | 50 | 1  | 42 | 74 | 34 | 66 |
| 67 | 27 | 59 | 10 | 51 | 2  | 43 | 75 | 35 |
| 36 | 68 | 19 | 60 | 11 | 52 | 3  | 44 | 76 |
| 77 | 28 | 69 | 20 | 61 | 12 | 53 | 4  | 45 |

## Formulating the Statement of Intent

This part is crucial, and you must be careful here. Don't use words like "I want"; instead of that, you should say, "I will, it is my wish, this is my will, I am," etc. I prefer, "I will." Example: I will make fifty thousand dollars a month. You have to be sure about what you really want. There is no space for doubts here, and you should never use negative words because your subconscious mind plays an important role here, and it tends to ignore all negative words. Instead of saying, "I don't want to be sick anymore," you say, "I will be cured." Otherwise, your subconscious would understand, "I want to be sick."

## Removing Vowels and Repeated Letters

To make the process easier, you should remove all vowels and repeated letters from your statement. You don't need to worry because your intent was already created, and the universe knows what this sequence of letters means. Example: "I will make fifty thousand dollars a month" will become WLMKFTYHSNDR.

## Converting Letters into Numbers

This process is called Gematria. There are many methods you can find on the internet, such as Hebrew, Latin, Crowley, Golden Dawn Hebrew, etc., but you just need the Agrippa Gematria, which is the most accurate method available.

## Table 18. The Agrippa Gematria

| A | B | C | D | E | F | G | H | I |
|---|---|---|---|---|---|---|---|---|
| 1 | 2 | 3 | 4 | 5 | 6 | 7 | 8 | 9 |
| K | L | M | N | O | P | Q | R | S |
| 10 | 20 | 30 | 40 | 50 | 60 | 70 | 80 | 90 |
| T | U | X | Y | Z | J | V | Hi | W |
| 100 | 200 | 300 | 400 | 500 | 600 | 700 | 800 | 900 |

Note that Hi is an obsolete letter.

## Reducing Numbers

The squares have a limited amount of numbers. If you have VZS in your statement of intent, which corresponds to 700-500-90 according to the Agrippa system and you are using the square of the Sun for example, you have to remove zeros till it fits. 700-500-90 would become 7-5-9.

How do we know the last number of each planetary square? Just multiply the horizontal lines by the vertical ones. Example: Sun = 6x6 = 36. So, with the Sun, you can only use numbers up to 36.

## Creating the Seal

Now you need to link the numbers on the proper square respecting the order of the sequence. If the first number is 5, so you start by 5. Make a circle in the first number indicating the starting point and a line in the last one indicating where it ends. If your sequence has consecutive repeated numbers, you can draw a hook showing that the line is passing through that number twice.

# Planetary Magic

| 6 | 32 | 3 | 34 | 35 | 1 |
|---|---|---|---|---|---|
| 7 | 11 | 27 | 28 | 8 | 30 |
| 19 | 14 | 16 | 15 | 23 | 24 |
| 18 | 20 | 22 | 21 | 17 | 13 |
| 25 | 29 | 10 | 9 | 26 | 12 |
| 36 | 5 | 33 | 4 | 2 | 31 |

**Figure 37. Drawing a planetary seal**

On a blank sheet of paper, draw two triangles one inside the other and draw the seal inside the smaller triangle, as shown below.

**Figure 38. Finishing a planetary seal**

The border of the two triangles and the seal must be drawn in the color of the planet. On the left outside of the smaller triangle, you write the name of God of the sphere, and on the right, the name of the archangel of the sphere. In the lower part of the smaller triangle, you write the name of the archangel of the planet; on the left side, write the name of the intelligence and on the right, the name of the spirit of the planet.

# Consecrating the Seal

This is an important step that can't be avoided. You must consecrate it in the hour of the planet, but it doesn't need to be at the same hour you made it because I doubt you would have time. For example, you can make it in the morning and consecrate it at night.

**Things you will need**

- A white candle.
- Incense (any type).
- A glass of water.
- Salt, soil, or sand.

**Temple arrangements**

I. Set up an altar in the center of the area in which you are working. It is a simple altar. You can use a box, a mini table, or anything where you can put things over it. There must be space for you to walk around it.

II. Put the incense on the ground in the east, the candle in the south, the glass of water in the west, and the salt (soil or sand) in the north.

**The ritual**

I. Put the seal on the altar.

II. Perform the Banishing Ritual of the Pentagram.

III. Perform the invocation of the four elements (see the Appendix).

IV. Go to the east, face east, and say:

> *The intention of this work is to consecrate a seal of [insert the name of the planet] to [say the intention of the seal]. So mote it be.*

V. Go to the west of the altar and face east. Point your wand at the seal. If you don't have a wand, use your right index finger. Say:

> O You who are [insert the name of God of the sphere], Almighty God of [insert the name of the sphere], bless this seal and let what it represents to manifest in my life.
>
> O You who are [insert the name of the archangel of the sphere], Mighty and Powerful archangel of [insert the name of the sphere], bless this seal and make what it represents to manifest in my life.
>
> O You who are [insert the name of the archangel of the planet], Mighty and Powerful archangel of [insert the name of the planet], bless this seal and make what it represents to manifest in my life.
>
> O You who are [insert the name of the intelligence of the planet], Mighty and Powerful intelligence of [insert the name of the planet], bless this seal and make what it represents to manifest in my life.
>
> O You who are [insert the name of the spirit of the planet], Mighty and Powerful spirit of [insert the name of the planet], bless this seal and make what it represents to manifest in my life.
>
> In the name of [insert the name of God of the sphere], through the work of those ruling the planet [insert the name of the planet], whose names are written on this seal, [say what you want to happen, the intention]. So mote it be. Amen.

Note that with God, we used the verb let instead of make. This is because once we got permission from one of the divine names, everything is easier.

VI. Take the seal and go to the east. Light the incense and say:

> May the powers of the air consecrate this seal.

Pass the seal through the incense smoke.

Make the same with fire (south), water (west), and earth (north). You don't need it, and you must not let the seal touch the flame. And using your finger, put only a little drop of water in the corner of the seal.

VII. Return to the east, raise your hands, and say:

*I thank you, O Lord of the Universe, for letting this work happen.*

VIII. Draw the Banishing Pentagram of Air in the east, Fire in the south, Water in the west, and Earth in the north (see the Appendix).

IX. Perform the Qabalistic Cross to finish the ritual.

# CHAPTER 10

# SELF-PROTECTION

No matter if you occasionally cast a spell or if you are an active witch or magician, you need to protect yourself. Threats can come from anywhere, including someone close to you or entities that you work with. Generally, If you follow the basic rules to work with spirits, they will not cause you any harm, and the worst they can do is to refuse to work with you. When it comes to people, you can't control their actions; you can't prevent someone from cursing you or putting a black magic spell on you. But what you can and must do is to prepare your aura to be able to block these unwanted energies. When you are ready for something, you will not be taken by surprise.

In this chapter, we are going to learn the best protection techniques against the dangers of the occult world. If you follow the tips given here, you can be sure that nothing bad sent through the spiritual world will reach you.

# Balancing Your Energy

Have you ever found yourself in a situation where you were off-balance? For example, when you are standing on the bus, you need to hold onto the handrails to prevent you from falling over or when you are drunk and can't properly walk. These are concrete examples, but the principle is the same with our aura. When your energy field is operating only in one direction, receiving or losing, it is off-balance. The same happens when your energy field is weak since it is not getting the energy it needs to keep things going right in your life. These changes are so significant that an advanced psychic can notice there is something wrong with your aura only by looking at you.

The consequences of an off-balance energy are many, and your life can turn into a complete mess. You can get sick, lose your job, go through hard times in your relationship, get depressed, etc. Most people don't even notice that maybe something is wrong with them because they are used to it since this is a process that tends to occur gradually. So, they see it as a bad phase instead of fixing the source of the problem.

## Banishing and Invoking

In some parts of this book, you are instructed to perform the Banishing Ritual of the Pentagram before and/or after a ritual. When used before any magical work, it is useful to tune the magician with the highest forces in the universe, bringing the Tree of Life into the aura. Crowley, in one of his books, shared some information about this exercise. The following quote explains exactly what I just said:

> *"The habitual use of the Lesser Banishing Ritual of the Pentagram (say, thrice daily) for months and years and constant assumption of the God-form of*

*Harpocrates (See Equinox, I, II and Liber 333, cap. XXV for both of these) should make the "real circle", i.e. the aura of the magus, impregnable.*

*This aura should be clean-cut, resilient, radiant, iridescent, brilliant, glittering. "A soap-bubble of razor-steel, streaming with light from within" is my first attempt at description; and is not bad, despite its incongruities."*

The BRP also can cleanse one's energetic environment of chaotic energies. The problem starts when you use it on a daily basis without any kind of invocation. You are banishing things from your life and not receiving any. So, to avoid this, you need to invoke first and banish twelve or more hours later, or banish first and invoke right away.

**Suggested practice**

In the morning: invoke the four elements. Instructions on how to do this can be found in the Appendix.

At night: banish the four elements (see the Appendix).

Perform this exercise three times a week if everything is going well in your life, and you want to keep it that way, or daily if you feel things could be a lot better or if nothing is working for you.

## Building a Shield Around You

When working with magic, one of the first things you learn is you must develop a strong visualization technique. A variety of exercises and rituals demand the magician to really see what they are doing. When you draw a pentagram in the air, you must see it there; even if you turn around, you know there is a pentagram right behind you. This is necessary because our mind has the power to manifest things in the physical and astral world. Of course, it is a lot more complicated to do on the physical plane because we have something called the Laws of Physics, but on the astral level, it is quite easier since there are no limitations there. In this exercise, we are going to use our mind to create a shield around our aura, working with some key colors.

**Colored cards**

Prepare some paper cards in gold, dark red, and violet. Alternatively, you can use images on your smartphone, tablet, or computer instead of paper.

Gold: this color will attract divine protection to you.

Dark red: you will be a stronger person, always ready to face any difficult situation.

Violet: this color must be visualized in flames. It will cleanse your aura of all negativity at all existing levels.

**Step by step**

I. Use each color on a different day. My suggested order is violet, gold, and dark red.

II. Choose a quiet place where you can deeply relax. Sit in a comfortable position.

III. Hold the target color in front of your eyes. Stare at it for five minutes. Then put the paper card or device aside, relax your body, and close your eyes.

IV. Visualize yourself in the center of an empty place. This place is in the color you are working with. The color in the form of abstract light begins to emerge from all directions coming directly to your body. This colored light is now surrounding your whole body.

V. Imagine as if you were charging your batteries with this light. Feel the energy flowing through you.

VI. Keep doing this exercise for ten minutes. Then you can open your eyes, and it is done.

Don't forget that when working with the violet color, you must visualize it as flames and not as light.

# Amulets

Amulets are objects of protection with names and symbols engraved on it, representing the forces in which the object is connected, offering protection to those who use it. One of the most famous amulets are the seals of Solomon, also called pentacles. I sometimes use the Fourth Pentacle of the Moon to protect me against evil sorceries.

I restored all the three pentacles presented here to provide them with a better quality since the manuscripts where they are from are more than 500 years old.

## Instructions for All Planetary Amulets

I. Drawing, copying, and consecration must be done in the hour of the planet.

II. Ideally, you should draw the amulet on a blank sheet of paper using the color of the planet, but you can make a copy of it using a xerox machine as well.

III. All amulets must be consecrated to the four elements before you can use them.

## The Third Pentacle of Jupiter

This will defend and protect you against all kinds of spirits, especially the ones you evoke.

Figure 39. The Third Pentacle of Jupiter

# The Sixth Pentacle of Jupiter

This protects against all earthly dangers.

Figure 40. The Sixth Pentacle of Jupiter

## The Fourth Pentacle of the Moon

This protects against all evil sorceries and from all injury to soul and body.

Figure 41. The Fourth Pentacle of the Moon

## Activating the Pentacles of Solomon

All three pentacles presented in this chapter must be activated each time you use them. You do this by holding the pentacle in one hand while reading the corresponding Bible verse.

The Third Pentacle of Jupiter: Psalm 125: 1.

The Sixth Pentacle of Jupiter: Psalm 22:16-17.

The Fourth Pentacle of the Moon: Jeremiah 17:18.

## CHAPTER 11

# CREATING YOUR OWN RITUALS AND SPELLS

The content of this book up to this point has served not only for you to apply it in your life, but also as a way of learning the magical arts. If you have carefully read all the previous chapters, you already have a complete notion of how a spell works and how to proceed to cast them. My goal with this work is not only to provide you with the cake recipe; I want you to be able to create your recipes because any witch can reproduce the steps described in a book of magic, but the best ones go beyond and create their steps.

The construction of a spell is summarized in three parts: objective, energy, and structure. The first step is to decide for what purpose we are creating a spell, which can be anything as long as it is possible to come true. For example, there is no point in trying to use magic to grow wings and fly because it would never manifest on the physical plane. The second step is the definition of what will be the source of energy used to make the spell work. This energy can come from the magician/witch through their semen or blood, you can ask for the help of higher and even lower entities, and use the force of nature and the universe as a whole. The most practical and common option is to work with some spirit who has the necessary abilities. The last step is the structure of the ritual that involves the arrangement of the temple, the appropriate items such as candles and incense, and other rituals used to strengthen the spell.

# Step by Step

## Objective

Love, money, beauty, health, sex, manipulation, luck, professional success, help with studies, keep enemies away, spiritual cleansing, breaking spells, divination, dreams, astral travel, etc. The options are many and not restricted to the ones listed here.

## Energy

Here we analyze what we want to manifest, the complexity, and the options available. I will give you some tips based on my experiences, but you don't need to strictly follow them. You can and should try other alternatives if you wish.

**For difficult objectives**

If what you expect to achieve is something complex that will encounter many barriers on its way to becoming a reality, for example, to make someone who doesn't love you to fall in love with you, always seek the help of a higher entity. A higher entity means a more evolved spirit, not necessarily a "good" one.

Some demons are superior beings given their level of importance on the astral plane, examples: Asmoday, Azazel, Aim.

In this category of superior entities, we also include the gods (Greeks, Norse, Egyptians, etc.), planetary angels and archangels, and the Olympic Spirits.

**For less complex objectives**

For problems that can theoretically be solved more easily, superior spirits can also be used, and I only use them regardless of the situation. However, minor spirits can also handle it, such as the elementals of the air, fire, water, and earth, familiar spirits, angels, and demons of lesser importance.

When working with inferior spirits, be sure to give them all the necessary instructions because they are not good at interpreting what is asked of them. What you say to them is what they will do.

Your energy through blood and semen can also be used. However, I recommend that you use it only as a way of helping the entity with whom you are working with, giving it more power to carry out its task. Some spirits even ask for a drop of blood during the ritual. When this happens, their goal is not to harm you, but only to improve the efficiency of the work.

**The abilities of the spirits**

All spirits have specific abilities they are known for. Most will not accept to collaborate with anything that is not part of their nature. Gods and kings can do anything, but even they have some specialty in which they prefer to work with. For love spells, for example, look for Aphrodite, Freya, Isis, Frigga, Lilith, and others with this characteristic. Money and prosperity: Bethor, Seere, Bune, Fulla, Demeter, etc.

## Structure

I. Research everything about the entity you have chosen to work with and find out all the aspects of candles, incense, planet, best day and time to call it, etc.

II. Create an opening for the ritual that involves the preparation of the temple, altar, consecration of objects, banishing, meditation, etc.

III. Write at least two conjurations: one for the invocation and other with all the instructions you will give the spirit.

IV. Make a list of possible offerings that may include food, objects, public thanks, etc. I always recommend to publicly thank the spirit in internet posts, flyers, etc., because this is more useful to them than physical things. However, it is worth mentioning that regardless of what is offered, the spirit can always refuse it and ask for something different.

V. Create the final part of the ritual, such as thanks, instructions on what to do with the offerings, banishing, etc.

**Example of the basic structure of a spell**

I. Purification of body and soul by going without eating meat and having sex, bath, clean clothes (preferably white), etc.

II. Preparation of the temple: physical and spiritual cleansing (banishing), setting up of the altar with candles and incense, consecration of objects.

III. Declare the temple open, light candles, draw a magic circle.

IV. Preliminary conjuration.

V. Offerings and instructions.

VI. Final thanks and banishing.

# CHAPTER 12

# COMMON QUESTIONS AND SOLUTIONS

### Why didn't my spell work?

Well, it can be for many reasons. You may not have cast it correctly or provided enough energy for it to work. You must also consider that something in your life is blocking it, including past life issues. Try using the Violet Flame in your aura to cleanse you of all karma you may have from this life and the past ones.

### How long does it take for a spell to start working?

Immediately after cast, but there is a difference between when a spell starts working and when you see the effects. Depending on the problem you are trying to fix, it can take a month or more for you to notice anything.

## After evoking a spirit, I feel my life is getting worse. How can I fix this?

If you ask a spirit for general help like "I want to be happier," it will mess with your life. It happens because what you think is the best for you is different from what an entity thinks it is. So, always ask for specific things. To get rid of the influence of spirits, use one of the banishing rituals in this book, especially the Banishing Ritual of the Pentagram, and burn the seals of all the spirits you have been in contact with lately.

## Will I face the consequences of a black magic spell still in this life?

Who knows? It is completely possible. If you are worried about this, don't practice black magic or, at least, try not to do something really bad to anyone.

## Can spirits physically hurt me?

Yes, they can, but the ones described in this book will certainly not. In fact, this is not common at all. You can notice negative changes in your life, as already explained, but this is all.

## Some rituals in this book use names of God, do I really need to say them?

Those names are the manifestation of the highest forces in the universe. If we have spirits going from human souls to mighty kings, a higher power is above them all. This is logic. Many of these spirits are obedient to those names, so yes, you need to pronounce them.

## What can I do if a spirit refused to help me?

Did the spirit clearly tell you that? If yes, forget about it and move on. But if you think a spirit didn't help you because your spell didn't work, you have to consider that he couldn't do anything for you. In this case, try a different spirit.

## I performed an evocation, but I didn't hear, feel, or see anything. Did the spirit listen to me?

The fact nothing happened doesn't mean the spirit was not paying attention to you. You are just not ready, or you don't have any sensitive ability. It is very common, and you are not alone. In the Appendix, you can see how to develop your existing sensitive ability or try to acquire a small level of sensitivity.

## Can I replace the suggested incense and candles for the ones I have in my home?

If you want to use white candles, it is all right. White is a neutral color and can be used with any spirit. What you can't do at all is to replace a red candle with a yellow one, for example. Regarding incense, if you can't use the right ones, it is better not to use any. The exception is when you are trying to evoke an entity that you don't know much about. In this case, you can use any incense, but eventually, the spirit will tell you if he likes it or not.

# APPENDIX

# Invoking and Banishing the Four Elements

## The Qabalistic Cross

All the spheres of light in this ritual are formed from the same source of light. Other versions of it ask us to imagine those spheres without mentioning where their energy is coming from. I consider it a mistake, and that is why I created a modified version of the Qabalistic Cross.

I. Go to the east and face east. Stand with feet together and arms close to the body. Imagine that a sphere of brilliant white light is descending far from above your head. This sphere is about 10 inches or 25 centimeters in diameter, and now it is right just above your head.

II. With a dagger, wand, or your right index finger, touch the light and bring a fraction of it to the forehead. This smaller sphere is half the size of the one above your head. Touch the forehead and vibrate ATAH.

III. Touch the light again, but this time, point towards your feet and imagine the sphere of light descending to the ground. Vibrate MALKUTH.

IV. Now bring another sphere of light to the right shoulder. Touch the shoulder and vibrate VE-GEBURAH.

V. Bring another sphere to the left shoulder. Touch the shoulder and vibrate VE-GEDULAH.

# 142 Appendix

VI. Put your hands together in front of your chest and vibrate LE-OLAHM. Now clearly imagine the four spheres of light forming a cross and this cross entering your body, filling it with pure light.

VII. Still with hands together vibrate AMEN.

## Drawing the Pentagrams

Here you choose if you want to banish or invoke the four elements. The only difference is in the pentagrams you need to draw in this step. The following image gives you both the banishing and invoking versions.

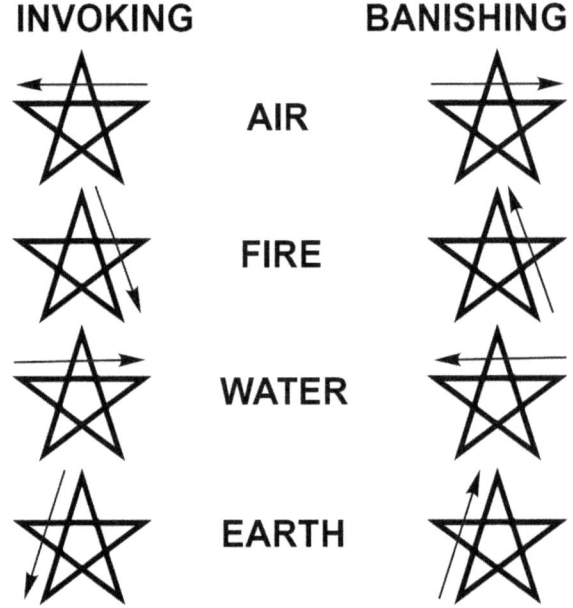

Figure 42. Invoking and banishing pentagrams

I. In the east, facing east, draw in the air the appropriate Pentagram of Air and then bring the point of your finger to its center. Vibrate the name YHVH.

II. Without moving your finger in any other direction, start tracing a circle while you move to the south. In the south, trace the appropriate Pentagram of Fire. Bring your finger to the center and vibrate ADNI.

III. Continue the semi-circle to the west and trace the Pentagram of Water, bringing your finger to its center. Vibrate AHIH.

IV. Repeat the same process to the north with the Pentagram of Earth. Vibrate the name AGLA ATAH GIBOR LE-OLAHM.

V. Now complete the circle bringing your finger to the center of the pentagram you drew in the east.

VI. Now in the east, stay in cross position (feet together and arms extended) and say:

*Before me, the great Archangel RAPHAEL (vibrate).*

*Behind me, the great Archangel GABRIEL (vibrate).*

*At my right hand, the great Archangel MICHAEL (vibrate).*

*At my left hand, the great Archangel AURIEL (vibrate).*

VII. Now say:

*About me, flame the pentagrams.*

Imagine the circle and the pentagrams in white flames.

*And in the column shines the six-rayed star.*

Imagine two hexagrams, one under and one above you, shining and forming a grid of light around your body.

VIII. Repeat the Qabalistic Cross, and the ritual is done.

# Developing Your Sensitive Abilities

These techniques will work better if you already have the necessary abilities, but they are not fully developed. On the contrary, you can achieve some level of sensitivity, but you will have to work harder on a daily basis.

## Exercise 1

I. Go to the internet and download any Shamanic meditation music. Transfer it to your smartphone or any other device where you can plug earphones.

II. Take three equal coins and mark them with any hydrographic pen. For example, write A, B, C. You can also use playing cards of different suits, credit cards, etc. The purpose here is to use objects with the same dimensions but with something different in each one of them.

III. Go to a quiet place and put three cushions in front of where you will sit.

IV. Take the three objects in your hands, close your eyes, and mix them. Still with eyes closed, put each object under a different cushion.

V. Sit down in a comfortable position, put on the earphones, and play Shamanic music.

VI. Close your eyes and relax. Think about one of the objects in front of you. Go through your mind under each one of the cushions and try to locate it. Take your time.

VII. When you are ready, open your eyes and check if you are right.

Practice this exercise daily until you guess right where the three objects are. Then you can start working with more objects until you are ready to locate them without the help of Shamanic music.

## Exercise 2

This exercise is called the Middle Pillar Ritual, and it helps to build the Tree of Life within the aura.

I. Perform the Qabalistic Cross.

II. Stand facing west, feet together, arms close to the body, and palms facing forward. On your right is the Black Pillar of Severity. On your left is the White Pillar of Mercy. You are in the middle representing the Pillar of Balance.

III. An incredibly bright white light, the Light of the Infinite-Self, originates far above your head.

IV. The light descends to the top of your forehead (Kether), forming a sphere the size of your head. Strongly vibrate the name: AHIH (pronounced "eh-heh-yeh").

V. Now imagine a shaft of light descending from your forehead to the throat region (Daath) and forming another sphere of light. Strongly vibrate the name: YHVH ALHIM ("ye-hoh-vah el-oh-heem").

VI. Now a shaft of light descends from your throat to the chest (Tiphareth), forming a new sphere of light. Strongly vibrate the name: YHVH ALOAH ve-DAATH ("ye-ho-vah el-oh-ah veh da-ath").

VII. Visualize a shaft of light descending from your chest to your genital region (Yesod) and forming a sphere of light. Strongly vibrate the name: SHADDAI AL CHAI ("shah-die el hai").

VIII. Finally, a shaft of light descends from your genital region to your feet (Malkuth), forming a new sphere of light that touches the floor. Strongly vibrate the name: ADNI HARTZ ("ah-doh-nye ha-rets").

IX. Now visualize the sphere at your feet rising and absorbing the light and energy of all the other spheres until it reaches your head. Now only one sphere exists. Imagine it circulating through your body from left to right. Keep doing it for three minutes, at least.

www.ingramcontent.com/pod-product-compliance
Lightning Source LLC
Chambersburg PA
CBHW070621300426
44113CB00010B/1605